Advance Praise for Josh Gordon's
Selling 2.0

"When your customers change, you change too. *Selling 2.0* is the most inspired and practical guide to dealing with the changing customer I have ever read. **Read it or be left in the dust!**"
—Lee Iacocca

"Learn from the experts! This book is full of powerful, practical, proven sales methods that help you to sell more effectively than ever before."
—Brian Tracy,
chairman and CEO,
Brian Tracy International, and author of *Maximum Achievement*

"*Selling 2.0* is a **powerful and illuminating** book. It is based on solid research that truly reflects what customers expect from salespeople today.... The author includes pearls of wisdom from a multitude of experts in the field that the savvy reader can turn easily into cash in today's competitive marketplace."
—Gerhard Gschwandtner,
publisher and editorial director, *Selling Power*

"Today, information and technological change continuously bombard companies, making the task of selling to them increasingly difficult. *Selling 2.0* provides salespeople with a comprehensive tool kit designed to help them work with companies to define a clear picture of where they are now and where they want to be in the future.... *Selling 2.0* is definitely required reading for successful selling in the new economy."
—Ed Grebow,
president of Sony's Broadcast and Professional Company

"Aggressive sales approaches simply won't work in a world where products and services are increasing commoditized and where customers are empowered by information technology and a global marketplace. **Josh Gordon offers an alternative approach that plays off customers' strengths rather than probing for weaknesses.** Instead of manipulating customers with techniques for overcoming objections and high-pressure closes, Gordon offers a step-by-step plan for building customer relationships through shared vision, shared knowledge, and trust."
—William Keenan Jr.,
editorial director, Alexander Communications Group
(publisher of *Sales Rep Advisor*)

"**Josh Gordon's book should be required reading for every employee in every company in America from the CEO down.** It is not about selling per se—rather it is about the relationships required for success in this info-tech environment where every day is a 'learn as you go' experience.... In my judgment, you cannot read this book and fail to be absolutely convinced that success in the new millennium will require that you change the way you have thought about your customers and how you have organized to serve them."
—Lou Pritchett,
former vice president, Sales, Procter & Gamble

continued on next page . . .

"*Selling 2.0* is the first book that captures the new thinking on selling in today's much changed economy. In this practical, step-by-step guide, **Josh Gordon challenges you with a new vision of the persuasion process. . . . Dale Carnegie, meet Bill Gates.**"
—David C. Hirsch, marketing director, Synergy, Inc.

"*Selling 2.0* takes a timely look at motivating customers to buy, which is paramount to selling in the new economy. Through case studies, analysis and common sense, **it challenges everything you have ever heard or read about sales.**"
—Evilee Thibeault, president and publisher, Network World, Inc.

"Customers are more demanding than ever. Luckily sales professionals have Josh Gordon to turn to for help. *Selling 2.0* offers vital insights into how to sell and market more effectively in the twenty-first century."
—Geoffrey Brewer, editor in chief, *Sales & Marketing Management*

"I strongly recommend Josh Gordon's new book *Selling 2.0*. **Gordon provides an effective, innovative paradigm for selling to customers in the new economy.** The rules have changed. The seller needs to adapt and assume the role of a motivator."
—Doron Kempel,
vice president and general manager, Media Solutions Group, EMC Corp.

"I read Josh Gordon's *Selling 2.0* with a mounting sense of excitement. **It is more than just a useful response to the challenges of selling in the new community—it is an inspired new way of relating to customers and their needs.**"
—Diane McCurdy, president, McCurdy Financial Planning

"Josh Gordon has written a terrific follow-up to *Tough Calls*. The author who taught salespeople to triumph in every possible sales difficulty now wants to help us take it to the next level. His new book moves the reader from old, traditional sales wisdom to new techniques of success. . . . *Selling 2.0* **is perfect for salespeople who are confident about today's sales—but who want to ensure tomorrow's.**"
—Katie May, editor, *The Competitive Advantage*

"Josh Gordon shows unusual insight into the changing world of sales and gives powerful guidance into how to accomplish sales performance. *Selling 2.0* will make a genuine and far-reaching contribution to most every reader's thinking and results."
—Ed Satell, president, Progressive Business Publications (publisher of *The Selling Advantage*)

"This is not a tough call—*Selling 2.0* is a groundbreaking book. Essential reading for any salesperson."
—Bob Rosner,
nationally syndicated columnist and author of *Working Wounded* and *Boss's Survival Guide*

"*Selling 2.0* clarifies just how radically the selling function has changed and provides practical, street-level strategies for success. **Read it before your competition does!**"
—Larry Wilson,
coauthor of *The One Minute Sales Person* and *Changing the Game: The New Way to Sell*

SELLING 2.0

Motivating
Customers
in the
New Economy

JOSH GORDON

BERKLEY BOOKS, NEW YORK

This is an original publication of The Berkley Publishing Group.

SELLING 2.0

A Berkley Book / published by arrangement with the author

PRINTING HISTORY
Berkley trade paperback edition / October 2000

The Penguin Putnam Inc. World Wide Web site address is
http://www.penguinputnam.com

ISBN: 0-425-17649-5

BERKLEY®
Berkley Books are published by The Berkley Publishing Group, a division of Penguin Putnam Inc., 375 Hudson Street, New York, New York 10014. BERKLEY and the "B" design are trademarks belonging to Penguin Putnam Inc.

PRINTED IN THE UNITED STATES OF AMERICA

10 9 8 7 6 5 4 3 2 1

*For Mom, who never stopped
believing that one day her
dyslexic son would learn to read*

Contents

Acknowledgments

The vision that started this book came to me quietly as I sat in my New York sales office late one afternoon pondering a simple question, "What did I do today to bring in business?" Even though I had had a full day of customer contact, it occurred to me that I had spent little time on the three activities most often synonymous with the selling process: pitching, overcoming objections, and closing. Instead, I had helped several clients see a new market opportunity, raced to e-mail some hot industry news to a few other clients before they could hear it from anyone else, helped a former client become a new one by finding him a job, worked out a value-added program with a client, started a research project for another client, and come up with an idea to help yet another client solve a distribution problem. As I thought back to how I did the same sales job ten years ago, I realized that I was now spending far less time "pitching and closing" and far more time on activities that instead motivated customers to buy from me.

I became obsessed with the question: "How do you motivate customers to buy from you?"

A month later, while speaking before a convention of experienced magazine space salespeople, I diverged from my prepared speech and asked this group my question. I had hoped for the enthusiastic embrace of a fresh new idea but instead faced blank stares and confused looks. Being a "customer motivator" sounded too abstract; it was not how these salespeople were used to defining their job. Then, even worse, several hands shot up and some well-intentioned individuals jumped into a canned product pitch. I said, "No, I'm not interested in how your product is better than your competitors', I want to know what you do, say, believe, or create that makes a customer WANT to do business with you and not with someone else." I left the podium feeling somewhat defeated, but better able to define my vision.

While being a "customer motivator" can sound abstract, I know in the field it is very real. I have struggled with clients who were motivated to buy from competitors and have worked hard to win over others who became motivated to buy from only me. It takes hard work to develop this kind of preference and loyalty among customers but, once established, when it's encountered in the field, it's as abstract as a brick wall.

As I conducted the first few interviews for this book, I began to uncover something beneath the surface that had not been articulated before. In a changing economy, where more of the power in the buyer/seller relationship was shifting to the customer, top salespeople were intuitively developing new approaches and revising old ones to be more persuasive with their customers. But these new approaches were not being widely shared because they were assumed to be too industry-specific or customer-specific.

With more interviews, patterns emerged that challenged this assumption. If these approaches were industry-specific, why then had Fidelity Investments' Steve Cone, Bristol-Myers Squibb's David Fortanbary, and The Microsoft Network's David C. Caffey all advocated the same approach? Since selling financial services, pharmaceutical products, and Web partnerships are generally considered different businesses it became clear that something deeper was going on.

With more interviews these patterns further developed and I began to see them not as isolated approaches, but as basic motivational strategies common to any selling situation in the new customer empowered, networked marketplace.

As I realized I was on to something bigger than my personal selling experience could fully explain, I pursued personal interviews with the brightest individuals I could find, representing every conceivable selling situation, at a wide variety of innovative companies.

Somewhere along the way, with the help of hundreds of people, the private vision created to further my personal selling goals had evolved into a global template for change. Many important people took time out of their busy schedules to be interviewed for this project. They deserve thanks.

Thanks to the high profile sales masters who supported this project, especially Lee Iacocca, Ted Turner, Brian Tracy, and Guy Kawasaki.

Thanks to those from the hi-tech world, including: Jeff Raikes, group vice president of worldwide sales, marketing and support, Microsoft; Dennis Reker, director of marketing operations for the Americas, Intel; John Kinnaird, vice president and general manager, Preferred Account Division, Dell Computer; Bill Etherington, senior vice president & group executive, Sales & Distribution, IBM; Gary Daichendt, executive vice president Worldwide Operations, Cisco Systems; Mark Jarvis, senior vice president, Worldwide Marketing, Oracle; Frank Pinto, vice president, Worldwide Sales, Sun Microsystems; Frank Coleman, vice president, AT&T Accounts, Lucent Technologies; Joe Valenti, senior vice president, Xerox Business Services; and Conrad Coffield, vice president, Broadcast & Production Sales, Sony Broadcast & Professional Company.

Thanks to those from service organizations, including: Bruce J. Himelstein, senior vice president of sales, North America, Marriott; Steve Cone, president, Customer Marketing & Development, Fidelity Investments; Richard Sweet, senior director of marketing and sales, Southwest Airlines; Joel Rossman, vice president, Sales, UPS; Robin Blunt, vice president, Global Marketing Programs, MasterCard; Allen Jones, senior vice president & director of marketing, US Private Client Group, Merrill Lynch; Bill Beckley, executive vice president of agencies, Northwestern Mutual Life; Joe Uva, president, Turner Entertainment Group Sales & Marketing; and Mike Peters, director of sales & marketing for the Americas, PricewaterhouseCoopers.

Thanks to those from Internet organizations, including: Paul Corvino, vice president & general manager, America Online Interactive Marketing; David C. Caffey, director of development, The Microsoft Network; Jeffrey Zink, eastern regional vice president, Yahoo!; Scott Schiller, senior vice president advertising & sponsorship sales, GO.com (Disney online); and Whit Andrews, senior editor, *Internet World*.

Thanks to those from companies leading change in their respected industries: Tom Moore, senior vice president of sales & general manager, Fountain Division, Coca-Cola; Jim Schroer, vice president, Global Marketing, Ford Motor Company; Tim Joyce, vice president, Global Sales, Nike; Cam Bishop, president, Intertec Publishing, Primedia Corporation; Forest Harper, vice president sales, Roeing Division, Pfizer; David Fortanbary, director of cardiovascular marketing, Bristol-Myers Squibb; Marty Sunde, managing director, Sales and Marketing, Enron Energy Services Operations, Inc.; and Ken McDonald, senior vice president, managing director–The Americas, Amway Corp.

Thanks to members of the Million Dollar Roundtable who added perspective on selling services from a small business perspective: Sidney Friedman, president, Corporate Financial Services; Diane McCurdy, president, McCurdy Financial Planning, Inc.; Marvin Feldman, president, The Feldman Group; Mike Weintraub, president, Contemporary Pensions; and Fran Jacoby, president, The Jacoby Agency.

Thanks to "Consultative Selling™" guru Mack Hanan and "SPIN Selling" guru Neil Rackham, the two "thinkers" of the selling profession. Their respective works, *Sales Shock!* and *Re-thinking the Sales Force* set the stage for this book. Rackham was especially enthusiastic about the project and encouraged me to pursue it by telling me that a practical, street-level guide to the changing sales profession would be the perfect complement to the "big picture" work already in print.

Thanks to Gerhard Gschwandtner, publisher & editorial director, *Selling Power* and Doug Chaney, publisher of *Sales & Marketing Management*, who approved me using their magazine's mailing lists for the research found throughout this book and in the appendix. Also, thanks to Dun & Bradstreet for providing the list that represented the buyer's perspective.

Thanks to Anna Fredericks of the Canadian Professional Sales Association who took extra time to help make my questionnaires more "real world."

Thanks to Timothy B. Spears whose detailed historical book, *100 Years on the Road*, introduced me to the world of selling between the years 1830 and 1930. As a result, thanks to A. Emerson Belcher, William H. Mather, and George L. Marshall for their inspired writings of their experiences in the late 1800s as "Commercial Travelers" (what traveling salespeople were called back then). A perspective on what selling was like at the turn of the nineteenth century helped me to write about what is truly different about selling at the turn of the twentieth century.

Thanks to the one hundred–plus people whom I interviewed personally and whom you will find quoted throughout this book, as well as the hundreds of people who responded to my surveys.

Finally, thanks to my loving wife, Lynn, who gave me daily encouragement during the months of manuscript preparation. As the former editor of *Marketing Communications* magazine she provided constant, invaluable perspective and advice. And thanks to Laura (age 10) and Jenny (age 6) who did without their dad for too many evenings and weekends during the course of this project.

It has been an exciting journey. To those who helped me along the way, thank you.

Introduction

"For a long time there was a feeling among salespeople that they had a bit of the upper hand in dealing with customers. But now it's come to a point where customers say, 'I dictate a little bit more to you than you dictate to me.' "

ANDY COHEN, executive editor,
Sales & Marketing Management magazine

Are you ready to sell to the empowered customers of the new economy?

In 1997 I encountered a buyer unlike any other I had met before. Through consolidation and acquisitions this client now controlled about 30 percent of the buying for the entire industry I was working in. After his company acquired yet another of its competitors, I was told I would lose all my business with them. I had to get them to change their minds. But how?

I offered to buy lunch, but my customer told me she didn't have time and, besides, letting a supplier buy her lunch was against company policy.

I told her my product's features were better than those of the products she was currently buying. She told me she didn't think our products were all that different.

I told her about better pricing for certain volume levels and arrangements I could offer her. She told me she could get great pricing anywhere.

I told her my company had a reputation for great after-sale service. She said all her suppliers offered great service.

Welcome to selling in the new economy, where more powerful buyers are unimpressed with the tools of persuasion that have assured salespeople success for the past twenty years!

Some business consultants, citing this increasingly common scenario, have proclaimed the end of the need for a sales staff. I strongly disagree. What we have is the start of something new and exciting that will enhance the importance of the sales staff. But salespeople will need to learn to use a new set of persuasive tools. As customers gain more power in the buyer-seller relationship, a new approach to selling is needed. Rather than trying to "push" these empowered customers with closing and pressure techniques, the future will demand persuaders who can "pull," or motivate customers to buy. The mission of this book is to present a step-by-step guide to the motivational selling tools needed to win business in the new economy.

Customer motivation is the new key to persuasion for the new economy. While economic trends are making many traditional persuasive approaches less effective, they are also creating new opportunities that didn't exist just ten years ago. Back then, most approaches started with the product itself. A salesperson's job was to explain the value the product had for the customer.

But persuasion in a time when product features, service, and pricing are less unique every day requires a different approach. Today's top persuaders think about every interaction they have with a customer that would motivate that customer to buy, and craft an approach that starts with the customer, not the product. Instead of selling product specifics these persuaders are selling the overall value of doing business with their company or themselves. On any day they might be selling their business model, a system, an idea for change, or their brand. They might also be found sharing knowledge, creating customer experiences, or creating value. These are not theoretical approaches. This book will show you step-by-step how innovative companies are using these approaches today in order to build sales.

How does a "motivational selling approach" work? A motivational approach works differently than the "present and close" approach that assured success in the past. When you use a motivational approach successfully the customer comes to his own conclusion that he wants to do business with you, and closing can be redundant. Using a motivational approach may take more time to take hold, but once it does it typically sweeps all competitive product pitches away in its wake.

For example, consider how two salespeople each went after the same account. The first took a conventional approach. He asked good questions about his client's needs, gave a presentation that showed how his product's features offered benefits that met those needs, and then asked for an order.

The second salesperson used a motivational approach. Instead of asking about client needs, she asked where the client saw her business five years from now. Instead of presenting features and benefits, she presented her company's vision of how both their companies could be doing business more productively five years in the future. Instead of asking for a product order, she laid out a step-by-step plan outlining how her company could enhance the customer's business over that time period. Then she asked if the client wanted to start working for a more productive future, today.

To the customer the two competitive products being offered did not seem all that different. But when one salesperson shared a vision of how to help him achieve greater success in the future he was motivated to buy from that salesperson. This salesperson motivated her customer to buy by sharing a vision, the subject covered in chapter 1 of this book.

Six trends that will mandate your need for customer motivation strategies

What started as an isolated instance that I first encountered in 1997 has grown into a number of trends that are affecting selling everywhere. If these trends are not affecting your sales territory yet, prepare yourself, because they will.

1. YOUR PRODUCTS ARE GETTING LESS UNIQUE

> "It used to be that when we came out with a technical innovation we had eighteen months to sell it before a competitor would duplicate it. Now it happens in a year."
>
> FRANK COLEMAN, vice president,
> AT&T accounts, Lucent Technologies

Design and manufacturing technology have empowered companies to quickly duplicate unique product features a competitor might have. The availability of highly skilled temporary workers allows any company willing to spend money to duplicate almost any service. Companies once had three to five years to exploit an innovation before a competitor could "knock off" that feature. Today, unique features sometimes become commonplace in as little as six months.

How do you sell features and benefits in a world where unique features simply don't stay unique for long?

2. YOUR CUSTOMERS ARE CONSOLIDATING

According to the *Selling 2.0* survey of sellers and buyers conducted for the book:

- 24.7 percent of salespeople report losing business because a customer was acquired within the past twelve months.

- 18.1 percent of salespeople report losing business because clients consolidated their supplier base within the past twelve months.

In many markets and industries, customers or distribution channels are consolidating, putting fewer large customers in control of an ever-greater percentage of buying in their industries. There used to be thousands of neighborhood toy stores throughout the country. In 1998 two companies, Toys "R" Us and Wal-Mart, accounted for just over one third of all toy sales made in the U.S. This phenomenon is not limited to retail. In the future you will have fewer, larger customers to sell to.

If you are maintaining a "the more calls you make, the more sales you make" mentality, how will you be successful when 35 percent of your business is controlled by three accounts?

3. YOU ARE GETTING MORE BUSINESS FROM ONGOING CUSTOMER RELATIONSHIPS

According to the *Selling 2.0* survey of sellers and buyers, an average of 70.2 percent of a salesperson's business now comes from repeat business.

In the new economy there will simply be less "one-shot" selling. "One-shot" sales are not profitable enough to maintain a personal selling relationship and so companies are moving these onetime transactions toward electronic commerce or call centers. Face-to-face salespeople will pursue longer-term sales relationships.

How do you hard-close for a sale today when you want an order from the same customer next month, next year, and into the future?

4. PRICE FLATTENING IS A REALITY

Customer consolidation, the emergence of large buying groups, and buying on bid over the Internet have forced many companies to offer lower prices. As lower prices become commonplace, price flattening results. "Price flattening" means that the price any customer pays, regardless of his buying volume, will become closer to the prices all your customers are paying.

5. YOUR CUSTOMERS HAVE MORE INFORMATION

The Internet has put the power of information into the hands of customers. It is not uncommon for salespeople to encounter customers who know as much about their product as they do. If you work for a publicly held company, anyone can mine a tremendous amount of information about you, your company, your products, and your competitors with a few judicious clicks of a mouse. Clients who know your weaknesses and strengths are going to be more demanding negotiators.

How do you ask your client if she "wants to buy a red one or a green one" when she's been on your competitor's Web site and realizes she can buy the same product in pink, blue, and yellow, too?

6. THERE IS AN OVERSUPPLY OF PRODUCTS

Years ago, when you sold a truly unique product or service, there was a sense of scarcity about it that you could use to close the sale: "Our monthly production is limited," "We only make so many of them a month," or, "We can only service so many customers in a year, so you better get your order in." Today, almost any product can be bought through international sourcing. Even services are being internationally sourced: U.S.-based word-processing work is being beamed to Ireland via satellite and cartoon animation is being done in Taiwan.

How do you close on scarcity when a product similar to the one you're selling is available from several domestic and overseas sources?

A renaissance in selling discovered

This book started with a question I pondered while working as a salesperson based in New York City. As I encountered smarter and more powerful customers who could not be pushed or pressured into buying, I began to ask myself: "How can I motivate my customers to buy from me?" As this project unfolded I asked this question of others in six surveys, over one hundred personal interviews, and as part of a massive 2,500-piece mail survey.

After my first few interviews I realized I'd hit upon something extremely important and pervasive. Figuring out how to motivate customers to buy is the key to every salesperson's success in today's customer-empowered marketplace.

Early on, a few people expressed surprise when they heard that the author of *Tough Calls,* one of the most practical hands-on books on selling, was writing a book that sounded "soft" or theoretical. I realized that if my vision of describing "customer motivation" was to become real, it had to be specific, actionable, and "real world." While *Selling 2.0* is as real world as it gets, there may be readers who do not recognize the world it describes.

In one survey I asked salespeople which motivational approaches they found most persuasive. I also asked customers to rate how these same approaches looked from the buyer's side of the desk. Contrasting the attitudes of salespeople and customers showed me a world where customers have changed a lot, while the attitudes of salespeople have lagged behind. A world where customers are far more open to the motivational approaches described in this book than most salespeople would believe. The survey also described a place where customers are simply not influenced by approaches many still tout as contemporary.

If you dwell on the number of persuasive sales tools that have lost their punch, you can get pessimistic. In contrast, my experience in discovering innovative new approaches to persuasion has been a reason for excitement. Over the course of conducting one hundred personal interviews I was dazzled at the quantity of great new ideas innovative salespeople everywhere were developing in relative isolation from each other. Collecting these new ideas into a book has been exhilarating; viewed together, these ideas point to a renaissance! If you are willing to embrace change, then there has never been a more exciting time to be in sales. As more people grasp the meaning of becoming a "customer motivator," the renaissance of new ideas will grow. "Customer motivators" will become far more involved with their customer's business, use far more creative approaches, and have more varied and interesting jobs than salespeople of just a few years ago.

Let the renaissance begin for you. Read on!

Motivating Your Customer by
Sharing a Vision

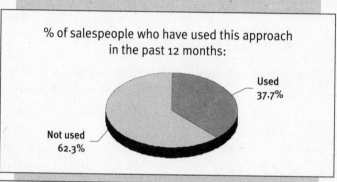

% of salespeople who have used this approach
in the past 12 months:

Used
37.7%

Not used
62.3%

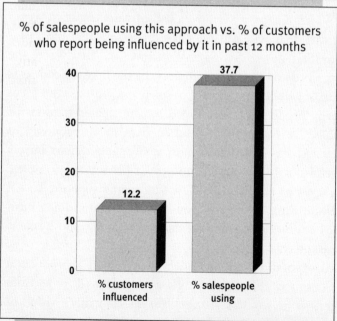

% of salespeople using this approach vs. % of customers
who report being influenced by it in past 12 months

37.7

12.2

% customers
influenced

% salespeople
using

"Ten years ago a lot of selling was about dealing with issues that came up in real time, but the pace of every industry is faster now. Today, selling is more about looking far into the future with your customers and working closely with them to solve mutual problems that may not exist yet."

DENNIS REKER, director of marketing
operations for the Americas at Intel Corporation

"I skate for where the puck is going to be, not where it has been."

WAYNE GRETZKY, possibly the greatest
hockey player of all time

Jeff Wattenmaker, a Silicon Valley software engineer, writes software that will run on microprocessors that are faster than any that now exist. Says Wattenmaker, "If I wrote the software to run on today's equipment, by the time the code was complete, it would run on slow, obsolete microprocessors." Today, many products get developed for anticipated markets or conditions. Buying products and services in an economy of rapid change has never been more challenging. Smart buyers are careful not to get locked into inflexible services, obsolete technologies, or products that lose service and support. To sell these future-wary customers, you must talk about doing business in the future in a way that motivates them to do business with you today.

Sony Corporation's vice president of broadcast & production sales, Conrad Coffield used to get a lot of bored looks from customers as he would try to explain his company's vision of where things were going to be a few years out. "But now things have changed," says Coffield. "There's a real interest in what the future will look like. Customers are used to the idea of constant change. Even if they don't work in a technology field, everyone has been acclimated to the idea of constant change because of exposure to the retail computer industry." With change a constant, helping buyers understand the future potential your products offer is critical.

OLD THINKING	Sell the product you have today, and let the future take care of itself. After all, you've got to eat today.
WHAT'S DIFFERENT	In a time of constant change, buyers are wary of buying products, systems, or services that may become obsolete.
NEW THINKING	To make a sale today, explain how you are preparing to respond to your customer's business needs five years from now.

Approaches

PAINT A PICTURE OF THE FUTURE

"When we talk to executives right now, our first approach is to go in and scare the hell out of them," shared Mark Jarvis, senior vice president of worldwide marketing for Oracle Corporation. Jarvis is convinced that most executives do not appreciate the impact that the Internet will have on their future business. Jarvis is a master storyteller who uses a series of short catchy ideas to paint a picture of a future where companies that buy into Internet commerce are big winners and those that do not could pay the ultimate price. Said Jarvis, "Let's go five years into the future. We believe there will be airlines with no planes. If you want to fly to London you will go to the Internet Airlines Web site, which will book your flight, send you a ticket, and send you a nice Internet Airlines brochure. The service will be excellent and everything will be nicely packaged. When you turn up at the gate to get on your plane, you'll be flying United." The idea of a Web-based booking service presenting itself as a full-service airline might be interesting for some, but if you are a travel agent or run an airline it could be terrifying.

Jarvis continued, "Probably the most famous example of this is Amazon.com. Now, Amazon.com may be the name of a company, but I think it should also be a verb. It describes what happens to a traditional company when a new Internet-based company uses technology to outflank its competitors. I was in the Asia Pacific region last week and I told every customer I saw that the Internet was going to change their business. My next statement was I'm willing to put money on the fact that if you take a look at the Fortune 500 companies today, in ten years' time a majority of those companies will no longer be in the Fortune 500. Why? Because they're going to be Amazon.com'd!"

Jarvis concluded, "After creating some fear and uncertainty in the customer's mind, we then go on to the things that we can do to help a company change."

DESCRIBE A PRAGMATIC MODEL FOR CHANGE

Jeff Raikes, group vice president of worldwide sales, marketing and support at Microsoft Corporation, believes that it is possible to use technology to enhance business effectiveness by accelerating the flow of information throughout the organization. Raikes advocates presenting this vision in a functional way. "First we sketch out a vision as to how this is possible. But the real key is to make this vision tangible for the buyer. I

like to give them specific examples. I'll talk about a product
that we use within our company to accelerate a purchase ordering system and I talk about an actual situation where we
used the system in-house. It used to cost us $60 per transaction,
but using this new technology, it's down to less than $5 per
transaction. We're saving $1.6 million per year and then we can
redeploy about twenty to thirty people into different roles at
our company." After sharing details, Raikes moves on to specific ways to apply this vision to the customer. "First we sketch
out a vision, then we speak to them about general examples,
and finally, having made the example seem tangible, we move
into some fairly concrete business proposals specifically involving their company."

MATCH THEIR VISION

For another approach to sharing a vision, let's look at Forest
Harper, vice president of the Roeing Division at pharmaceutical
giant Pfizer, Inc. He matches his company's vision with the vision of the company he's calling on. Says Harper, "If you
haven't yet established a relationship with a customer, you
could start by looking at their annual report or Web site to
discover what their mission statement is or goals are for the
next five years. You would look for parallel interests or parallel
alliances that your company might have and align these and
share this with your customer." This might sound pretty abstract to salespeople not used to this kind of top-down approach. But when you think about it, the vision statement a
CEO or the president of an organization creates is the lead that
everyone in the organization follows. In a well-run company
with strong leadership, values and direction flow, or are at least
articulated, from the top down.

Harper shared an example. "Say you're calling on a hospital
whose goal this year is to reduce the cost of a day's stay. We

would look at our own company and examine ideas and practices that we have where we share the same kind of goal. At our company we're always interested in trying to drive down extra costs. We have a variety of products and services we can offer this company to help them meet this kind of vision being set for the organization as a whole."

Harper told me that this approach is especially helpful when his sales team is dealing with a large organization and selling on several levels. Vision matching can keep the team moving in the same direction even though they are calling on different people and addressing different issues.

I find Harper's approach extremely effective with small businesses. I have called on many mom-and-pop companies where if you can align your vision with the mom or pop in charge, you can foster a very deep and personal bond.

HELP THEM DEFINE THEIR OWN VISION

"There's no more powerful motivational force than helping a customer clarify his own personal vision of where he wants his company, and himself, to be five years in the future," says Diane McCurdy, president of McCurdy Financial Planning, Inc.

Said McCurdy, "Often your job is to help clarify just what it is or where they want to be five years down the line. Once that vision is clarified, then you can present them with a series of options and choices that will help them get to where they want to be. Sometimes it means presenting them with difficult choices, even making them temporarily angry as they realize that they can't have it all."

I once made a call on the president of a small engineering firm who told me he wanted to run ads in my magazine because he saw that a competitor had. I could have quickly taken his money but felt I wanted to help him clarify what he really wanted to accomplish with his advertising. I started by asking questions. "What do you want to communicate and to whom? Do you want to generate sales leads, build a brand, introduce a new product, or just meet your competition in the market-place?" As he answered I didn't tell him what I thought he should be doing. Instead, I helped him clarify what it was he wanted to do. Three hours later I left his office with a client who had a clear vision of what he wanted to accomplish as well as an order. It was a good thing I took the time to do it. Two months later the competitor who had made him want to advertise in the first place stopped running ads. But my client, who had his own vision of what he wanted to accomplish, continued. Once a personal vision is set, there is no need to push the customer. Instead, the clarified vision does the pulling. Your job is to provide expertise that helps clarify that vision.

SHOW THEM OPPORTUNITIES TO TAKE ADVANTAGE OF

In the early nineties, the market for selling professional equipment to TV stations crashed when the Federal Communications Commission stated vaguely that all TV equipment would be redesigned to digital specifications at an unnamed future date. Afraid of being stuck with obsolete equipment, TV stations stopped buying. I was selling ad space for a TV equipment magazine to manufacturers who suddenly couldn't sell any product to broadcasters. Everywhere I heard the same story. "Our customers aren't buying, why should we advertise?"

I created a report that identified nine new kinds of television facilities that had not existed before. Because they were non-broadcast they were not affected by the confusion at the FCC, yet these facilities were aggressively covered by my magazine. My report included address lists so an ambitious salesperson could call up and try to make a sale. One company took the presentation to heart. After I left the company president's office he held a meeting with his sales staff and had them canvas every lead. Two years later one sixth of the entire company's billing was derived from those leads, and the company became a good customer of mine.

Sometimes selling a vision is about helping to make opportunities tangible for your customers.

TALK ABOUT RISK

"You can't successfully sell a vision if you don't understand the customer's perception of the risk involved," says Jeff Raikes of Microsoft. "The goal in sharing a vision is to motivate a customer to buy into that vision and buy the resulting products or services needed." But inherent in selling a vision is getting your customer to take a leap of faith. If the risk seems to outweigh the benefits, the sale will stall. Sometimes it is easy to get caught up in the excitement of the vision itself and forget that there are practical matters in buying.

If you meet resistance but are not getting any specific objections, I recommend asking directly just how risky the customer thinks your proposal is. Once you possess an understanding of this, you can deal with it. Share with them stories of others who have bought into this vision, talk about the support your organization can offer if things go wrong, or address specific concerns that come up.

ASK THEM TO COME ON BOARD

Paul Corvino, vice president and general manager of interactive marketing at America Online, describes his sales staff as having a big mission: "We are not just selling Web banners, we are building a new medium. Our mission is to build a medium that will be more valuable to people than the telephone or television."

With a mission like that, Corvino believes his company is making history. "We are working at a time and a place that people are going to look back to and say this is where the template was built. We are selling people on the concept of this change and then presenting them with the opportunity to be a part of it with the organization that is leading the way."

Step-by-Step

Although sharing a vision is often done in a spontaneous style, it takes a lot of preparation and thinking.

1. CONSTRUCT A VISION STORY

Your job is *not* to present a detailed description of how things will be five years from now, but rather to provoke thought on the subject and present ideas in broad strokes. A vision story typically is light on detail. Your job is to present ideas in the big-picture framework and let your customer fill in the details as they relate to his business, his company, his product needs, his CEO's vision, etc.

The challenge is to come up with ideas that are credible, on target, and reflect a deep understanding of the customer's business. On occasion I have tried to wing it with terrible results. If you can bring something to the table that is insightful, most often a terrific dialogue results. If you show up with ideas that are off the point, the client will lose interest quickly. Many sales organizations share forecast research with their sales staffs. If yours isn't one of them, research trade magazines that cover your industry, do Web searches, or take an informal sampling of your customer base to come up with some plausible predictions about how things might be different five years from now.

2. ASK IF YOUR CLIENT IS PREPARING FOR THE FUTURE, AND IF SO, HOW

The future is many things to many people. During my interviews I heard a lot about "five years into the future," but some clients don't look so far ahead. The higher the level of the person you're calling on, the further away "the future" is likely to be. For company presidents, look five to ten years down the road, with general managers discuss what is coming in two to three years, and for professional buyers you might talk about what's coming next year. To gain this perspective ask some general questions:

How do you see your business changing in the future?

What are you doing to take advantage of the changes that are coming?

What trends do you see unfolding in your business over the next five years?

3. START WITH THE COMMONPLACE, THEN MOVE TO THE FUTURE

When the popular children's TV show *Sesame Street* was in development, its producers did some fundamental research in order to discover how children learn about abstract concepts like letters. They found that learning proceeded most quickly when an abstract concept like "the letter *J*" was described in terms of familiar tangible things. Thus, "They tell me that's the letter *J*, well, I think it looks like a fishhook."

The best way to explain a vision of the future is to start with something your customer understands extremely well and then to move it five years into the future.

When Mark Jarvis described his vision of Internet Airlines, he was sharing an experience that every business person understands, that of buying a ticket and getting on an airplane. Taking that commonplace experience and moving it five years out is what grabs your attention.

4. TALK ABOUT THEIR BUSINESS, NOT YOUR PRODUCTS

Selling a vision is about business procedure, not product detail. If you focus on the specifics of your product or service five years from now, it will sound like another product pitch and you'll lose your customer's attention.

If you sell bricks, talk about changes in building construction five years from now; if you sell advertising space talk about what marketing will look like in their product category five years from now. If you sell cars, talk about how transportation will look in five years; if you sell life insurance, talk about how a policy will fit into a person's overall financial plan five years from now.

5. UNDERSTAND THEIR BUSINESS TODAY BEFORE YOU PREDICT TOMORROW

Sometimes talking about the future is more about making points by demonstrating expertise than getting the predictions right. No one really knows what the future will look like, but if you can credibly talk about your customer's business with your facts straight, you will give your customers confidence that you and your company can handle any changes that come up. After a meeting you want them to say, "Hey, those people really have a fix on what is coming; if we buy from them we can't go wrong."

6. ADDRESS HOW THEY CAN PROTECT CURRENT INVESTMENTS

Says Frank Coleman, vice president of AT&T sales at Lucent Technologies, "You're just never going to get too far in selling a vision if you don't integrate the procedures for changes with the current situation. Buyers hate salespeople who come in and make outlandish comments about how different things will be without describing an upgrade path as to how to get there. You need both a vision of the future and a migration plan that tells you how to get there."

7. FOCUS ON MEANINGFUL CHANGE

If your client wants to take advantage of the vision you share, she will have to make changes and purchases to get there. Diane McCurdy, of McCurdy Financial Planning, suggests, "When you present changes a customer can make, be sure you're not talking about change just for the sake of changing. The change has to be meaningful. Some people like to jump on the latest bandwagon, but I think you have to look and say, okay, forget the hype, where will this position you? How will this help your business grow?"

8. MAKE THE VISION STORY STICK

It's one thing to tell a great story about the future. It's quite another to tell a story about the future that motivates a customer to take action. I have found that the way to really get people excited is for them to see an opportunity for themselves or their organization that they didn't see before. The best vision stories spark the imagination of your customer and drive your dialogue to places where new opportunities for your customer appear to be in reach. When your client sees new opportunities, true excitement builds and action results.

Reality Check

WHAT IF YOUR COMPANY DOES NOT HAVE A VISION?

According to Michael Brinkman, director of strategic business development for Panasonic Broadcast and Digital Systems Company, salespeople explain the company's vision to the markets they serve, but they can also help you shape them. Says Brinkman, "The people who are going to find out about changes in a market the quickest are the salespeople who are living out there. With things changing more quickly, smart companies rely on their salespeople to give them valuable feedback to help them formulate their visions of the future." If your company doesn't have a vision, try to gather feedback when you make your respective calls. On every call, ask your customers where they see their business going in the next five years. After a month or two of this, share this feedback with the home office.

WHAT IF THE COMPANY YOU ARE CALLING ON DOES NOT WANT A VISION?

Pfizer, Inc.'s Forest Harper suggests that, "If the customer you are calling on lives too much in the present to think about what his role might be five years out, instead of talking about visions, just talk about goals. Every individual and company has some kind of goals. Sometimes goals can be short term and sometimes they can be longer term, but by shifting the discussion from visions to goals, you can have a similar kind of discussion of a more concrete nature."

Application Question

How can I describe the future of my customer's business, five years from now, in a way that will motivate my customer to buy from me today?

2

Motivating Your Customer by
Sharing Knowledge

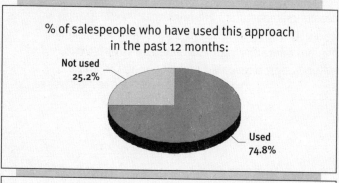

% of salespeople who have used this approach in the past 12 months:

Not used
25.2%

Used
74.8%

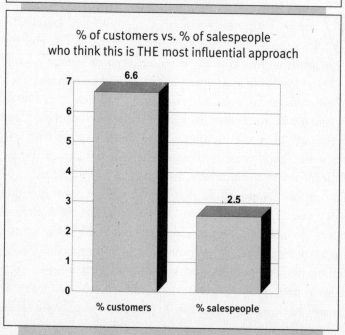

% of customers vs. % of salespeople
who think this is THE most influential approach

6.6

2.5

% customers   % salespeople

"Right now there is a proliferation of information. We think the competitive distinction you achieve as a company is not in the information you provide but in the judgment you exercise in using it."

ALLEN JONES, senior vice president, director of marketing,
US Private Client Group, Merrill Lynch

"Successful manufacturers are ones that invest strongly in education. If you put the effort into noncondescending training and educating your customers on your technology, they will be appreciative and reward you in the end."

KAREN LUKANOVICH, president, Simon River Sports

When I was training for my first sales job in the late 1970s, I was told that I could control any sales call by controlling the information about my product. My new employers told me, "Don't give your customer too much information because it will just cause confusion, and confused customers don't buy." They told me a large part of my job was limiting information. But with the arrival of the Internet, if you don't provide your customer with significant information, she will just click a mouse, find the information elsewhere, and take her buy with her.

The opposite approach is advocated by Mike Peters, director of sales and marketing for the Americas at Pricewaterhouse-Coopers. Says Peters, "Our ultimate goal is to open up our entire knowledge base to everyone in the business community, including our competitors and students." Peters likes to compare his approach of sharing information with the one taken by Microsoft back when the personal computer industry was in its infancy. Microsoft made the decision to share information on their operating systems with any software developer who asked for it. Competitor Apple Computer chose not to, and as the years ticked by Microsoft became dominant.

Sharing information gives you exposure and familiarity with a targeted customer base. According to Peters, it is natural for people who have a problem to solve to be motivated to work with people they have come to rely on for information in the past.

More change is coming according to Jeff Raikes, group vice president of worldwide sales marketing and support at Microsoft. "As information systems get more sophisticated, they will give companies the ability to open up to customers. This means that salespeople can focus on higher value-added processes instead of just flowing information to customers."

OLD THINKING	By controlling the flow of information to the customer, you control the sales call.
WHAT'S DIFFERENT	The Internet has put vast amounts of information within easy reach. Trying to control what information flows to your customer will only lose you sales and credibility.
NEW THINKING	Information is a commodity. Give away as much as you can to build credibility. Share the knowledge to put information to work to attract customer's interest and hold on to the sale.

Approaches

Today's formula for success is to give away as much information as you can to attract attention, build interest, and create credibility, then hold on to the sale by fielding salespeople with the knowledge to make the information actionable.

GIVE THE CLIENT CONTROL

While the old model of selling was to control information and tell the customer what he should buy, a very different model works well for Steve Cone, president of Customer Marketing and Development at Fidelity Investments. Cone aims to keep clients coming back by being a resource. He gives customers all the information and tools he can to manage their own finances and buy what they want. Says Cone, "Educating people is really the number-one role that we have here, and through it we give our customers a sense of control. With our help they get the expertise they need so they can manage their own finances as well as a professional could, as long as they spend time at it and don't get too fancy." Cone notes that when a customer needs special help, his people become the experts to contact but adds that, "The vast majority of time we try to make the customer the expert."

If you empower your clients to become better buyers, you are providing invaluable help. I know salespeople who resist offering this kind of service, thinking that if they create a smarter buyer they might be creating a more aggressive negotiator as well. I believe the potential gains are greater than the losses. I once helped educate a notorious price grinder, new to my market, on how to be the best buyer possible. As he asked me question after question about getting the best deals in my market, I swallowed hard and stayed true to my mission. When he did his buying I got a huge contract with very little pressure for rate concessions. I heard later that he used the information I provided to bash my competitors over the head for better pricing. To this buyer, what I had provided was worth the money.

SHARE APPLICATION KNOWLEDGE

When David Allen, now sales director of La Brea Bakery owned the Moon Dog Ice Cream chain, he bought a lot of products from salespeople. Recalls Allen, "I'd say 95 percent of the salespeople who called on me wasted my time, but one guy from a flavoring company I had never heard of became a great help. He came into one of my stores with no briefcase, no presentation, or anything to show me. Instead, he started by asking me questions. We had a very natural conversation about my ice-cream products and eventually he asked if he could taste them. Just by tasting my ice creams *he* told *me* which competing flavoring company I was buying from and just how much flavoring I was using to make my products. I was amazed. I figured anyone who can do that was worth listening to and if I bought from him I could improve my products."

Then Allen did what a lot of buyers do: switch suppliers to buy from a salesperson who offered application knowledge that made his products more appealing, more valuable, or more cost-effective.

MUSTER INTERNAL KNOWLEDGE

If you sell to sophisticated clients your company probably has substantial internal knowledge support to offer. At Bristol-Myers Squibb, David Fortanbary, director of cardiovascular marketing, explains, "We can provide clinical services that support physicians with high-level science information. For example, we might bring in someone who has specialized expertise in disease management."

When you are working with sophisticated information, the challenge is to understand the needs of your clients on a detailed level so you can channel internally generated information their way. Says Fortanbary, "Ten years ago we would walk in the door and say, 'Here's my product and this is why you should write it.' Today we have to get a lot more involved and we take considerably more time fact-finding. We need to understand our client's clinical issues as well as their economic issues."

Top salespeople who are good at mustering internal information for their clients are more than pass-through agents. According to Fortanbary, that's because they're so close to their customers and their needs that they become invaluable to the company's resource development programs.

USE HOMEGROWN INFORMATION TO BUILD CUSTOMER KNOWLEDGE

There is a huge amount of information available to salespeople who take the time to go on the Internet or make a few phone calls. It does not matter that this information is just as accessible to your clients. "New research" and "new information" in sales terms is simply research and information your customer has not seen before. Information gathered from common sources can have real impact if you share it in a way that encourages a dialogue.

I once sold advertising space for a tabloid trade magazine whose primary competitive advantage was that its ads generated more sales leads than its competitors' ads. As I started working this territory I thought the "more sales leads per ad" pitch would be a knockout sell, but found clients less than impressed. After a few months I started asking my clients how they handled their sales leads. With few exceptions, I found that the leads were not being taken seriously. A secretary would mail a brochure out when a lead arrived but there was no further follow-up.

I reasoned that if my clients got more sophisticated about handling their sales leads, they would value the leads more, and therefore value a lead-generating publication more. I did some Web searches, phoned a few companies, and dug up some articles. Over a three-year period I did the following:

1. Collected and shared about a dozen articles on setting up a lead management system.

2. Contacted lead management service companies, obtained multiple copies of their promotional packages, and shared them with my clients. Then I called the lead service company, gave their salespeople my client list, and encouraged them to call.

3. Compiled and shared a list of companies who provide the software to set up in-house lead management systems.

4. Obtained copies of in-house lead management software samples and shared them with my clients.

5. Became expert enough on one of these software packages to give product demonstrations to several of my clients.

Every time I visited my clients, developing a lead management system was part of the dialogue.

After my first year on this campaign, several of my customers gave serious looks at lead management systems. I encouraged them to talk to each other: "Hey, Marty, do you know what Carl is up to?" I would ask. Several did talk to each other and the peer-to-peer conversations helped move things along.

By the second year of my campaign I could walk into a new client's office and give him a highly customized, intense training program on how to set up a lead management system. I always left behind enough information on services appropriate for his organization so that he could take it from there.

Few of my clients actually followed the specific recommendations I made in my initial conversations. Most found their own ways to meet their specific needs and only two clients bought services from companies whose information I distributed. It was not my job to sell these systems, only to share knowledge on their value and hope they would be implemented. But after three years every major account in my territory did put in a lead management system, and when I left that sales territory billing had increased by 150 percent.

VIEW EVERY TRANSACTION AS A LEARNING EXPERIENCE

David Caffey, director of development at The Microsoft Network, observes, "The companies who have survived and will do well in the future view themselves as learning organizations. The companies that think they know everything or can do everything are the ones that are gonna be locked out." Caffey's job is to bring Internet content providers onto the Microsoft Network.

He describes part of this process as one of co-learning. Says Caffey, "Every time you do a deal you learn from the other company. When we start doing business we grow together in a business sense, but both organizations also learn about the other's business. This increases the knowledge base of each."

Step-by-Step

The essence of motivating your customer to buy by sharing knowledge is to become a knowledge resource that your customers come to rely on.

1. ASK, "HOW SOPHISTICATED IS MY CLIENT ABOUT INFORMATION?"

I once wowed an unsophisticated customer by simply visiting the Web sites of her competitors before I made a call on her. During my call I shared printouts of their most recent press releases. She did not realize this kind of information was easily available and thought she was getting some real inside information. Today, most of my clients regularly monitor their competitor's Web sites, so that kind of information doesn't generate much interest. With my most sophisticated clients I often work as a go-between with an in-house support department passing along very high-level expertise.

Where you start depends on how sophisticated your client is about information. The temptation with a less sophisticated client is to charge in and dazzle them. I have seen this approach backfire and caution against it. While it may be an ego trip to wow someone with your organization's brilliance, your aim is to build a relationship of trust that results in client action. Overwhelming your client can build real distance between you, and if the information you are presenting goes way over your client's head it may be viewed as an academic exercise instead of motivating them to take action. If you are dealing with less sophisticated companies, start the dialogue at their level but lead them forward.

It is usually easy to get a feel for how sophisticated about information your customers are. For hard-to-read clients take a look at how they gather information from outside sources. Ask yourself:

How well do they know their customers?

How do they get customer feedback?

How well do they understand you and your competitors?

How realistic are their evaluations of how they stack up against their competitors?

2. TARGET A KNOWLEDGE AREA AND LEARN IT

You job is not to become more knowledgeable than your client about her business, nor to become so knowledgeable that you start to tell her how to run her business. Your job is to be more knowledgeable about aspects of your client's business that are touched by your product or service and to become a learned expert on your customer's successful use of your product.

Given your product area, what does your client need to learn to become more successful? Once you know this, your challenge is to become a student of this area of information so you can offer expert advice.

It is possible that your industry has specific areas or trends to explore. If not, here are areas of interest where being an outside supplier can actually be an advantage:

A. Offer the perspective of your "average customer"

If you sell kids' costumes to party stores, you can assume that in October you are going to sell a lot of Halloween costumes. But how many more than in an average month? How are this year's sales ahead of last year's? By looking at your own internal information you might be able to come up with information on what direction your "average buyer" is going in. Contrast sales of this year with last year, this country with other countries, this year's convention versus last year's convention, this style line versus that style line, etc. To your customers, this kind of information regularly provided can help them understand if they are performing at optimum in their market segment.

B. Spot trends

Where are things going? According to Barry Nathanson, publisher of *Beverage Aisle* magazine, "In a day I talk to fifteen people from different companies, so I have a pretty good perspective on what's going on in my market. From these conversations I can give a generalized overview of the industry without ever betraying the specific trust of any one company.

"It helps me to talk in generalities about what is going on in the marketplace. For instance, I've been saying all year that this is a price-correction year and so all my beverage companies are scared because if Coke drops the prices again, there is a trickle-down effect. It affects everybody."

C. Help customers understand your category better

Before anyone buys a product from you, they first have to have an interest in your product category. If you are the one who takes the time to educate a newcomer about your product category and why it would be useful for their situation, you will have the inside track when the discussion shifts toward the topic of an actual purchase.

D. Spot success patterns

When I sold research studies I noticed that customers who were happiest with my custom survey work asked certain questions on their questionnaire. As I took on new clients I started suggesting we add these questions to their questionnaires, too. Whenever I work a territory I like to make note of customer behavior that results in success, whether it is related to my product or not. Successful customers usually buy more of whatever you are selling.

E. Welcome to the new job

If a new buyer replaces the one you have been dealing with, you have an opportunity to position yourself as a knowledge provider. I am surprised at how much basic information about their job new buyers lack. When I spot this situation, I try to fill the gap. I put away my product information and make an educational call. Typically the information I share is very basic: here is how the industry you are now in functions; here are the different product categories you typically buy; and here are the major suppliers. In addition, I am often able to share ideas on what the buyer's predecessor did that worked well and what didn't work.

3. PACKAGE INFORMATION FOR LEARNING

Mike Weintraub, president of Contemporary Pensions Inc., says, "I've noticed that the people who can communicate something that's complex in a very simple, straightforward way tend to get the business that others can't." A lot of being an information provider is about packaging the information so it can be easily digested.

A. Simplify

Says Paul Corvino, vice president and general manager of America Online interactive marketing, "We've got to make things simple and understandable for our customers. I don't even like my people using complicated words like the 'Internet' or 'e-commerce.' I want them to say, 'Let me show you how to sell things with a computer.' "

Customers who understand what you are selling become buyers. Most industries are infested with alienating jargon. Avoid it as much as possible.

B. Use word pictures

Marvin Feldman, president of The Feldman Group, often has to explain sophisticated financial tools to nonfinancial-services people. Says Feldman, "If I put a column of numbers before a client his eyes glaze over, so instead I try to paint a word picture so they can visualize what I'm talking about."

For example, Feldman sells a type of insurance policy for business partners that provides money in case something happens to one of the partners. The way this policy works is complex, so Feldman paints a word picture: "I call this a seesaw policy. You probably have never heard of a seesaw policy, but you know what a seesaw is. It takes two people to make a seesaw work. If one person gets off, what happens to the other person? He falls off. So I set up a seesaw policy so that when one person gets off—either from death, disability, retirement—a big chunk of money flows in, landing on the seesaw where that person was. No one falls off." Says Feldman, "Word pictures are helpful because my clients can visualize what a policy is going to do."

C. Make information visual

Mike Weintraub, president of Contemporary Pensions Inc., uses computer programs to generate visual graphics to make things more understandable. Says Weintraub, "It's easy to understand that if the blue bar is larger than the yellow bar, that's the way to go. This is an educational process and I think we've evolved into highly paid teachers."

4. GET CLIENTS IN THE HABIT OF LEARNING

Marty Sunde, managing director of sales and marketing at Enron Energy Services Operations, Inc., says, "After you make a sales call you want your client to go to their next staff meeting and excitedly say, 'Hey, do you know what I just learned?' " Sunde continues, "If you can't elicit that kind of response then you're going to fail."

The key to getting this kind of response is preparation. You need to focus on a subject your customer is very interested in, gather data that is as good or better than your client's own, and deliver it in a compelling way.

So what if you show up with data that the customer already has? I find that clients appreciate confirming internal data with an external source. If you share useful information on every visit, your clients will expect to learn something when you show up. A client once paid me a high compliment when he said, "Josh, whenever you come by for a visit I always learn something."

5. FINDING OPPORTUNITIES IN THE LEARNING DIALOGUE

The biggest win in sharing knowledge comes from jointly discovering new knowledge that can result in more business for both of you.

A magazine I worked for put on a seminar in the broadcast technology field just as digital television technology was being introduced. The attendees were chief engineers at TV stations and networks known for their technical ability.

As value added for a client, I conducted a survey on digital video technology at the seminar. My client donated the door prize of a camcorder to encourage participation and we conducted the survey the morning before the seminar began. When the survey came back we were shocked. The best technical minds of the analog television world did not have even a basic understanding of digital television.

Together we had discovered something new and both organizations benefited. My client went on to develop great digital products that would be more basic and user-friendly. My magazine introduced a new monthly column on the basics of digital television which soon became its most popular feature. My client signed on to run a monthly ad facing that column.

I have seen many salespeople waste their value-added resources on cash-based programs like promotional discounts or dealer incentives. I always advocate programs that build knowledge. These programs can disclose new information from which new business opportunities emerge that your competitors will never hear about.

Reality Check

WHAT IF MY CLIENT "KNOWS IT ALL"?

1. Ask yourself, "Have I earned the right to be an educator?"

You have to build credibility before you can be taken seriously as an educator. Sometimes it takes time to earn the respect of a customer.

2. Get past their ego

Some clients do not want to be taught, but still want to learn. The challenge is to find ways to present information that does not imply that they don't know a lot. I asked one client if I could "run some things by him that he probably already knew" before launching into an explanation. By his questions and reactions I could tell that he had a lot to learn, but his ego was just too big to admit it. My approach saved face for him and we both learned something.

Another approach is to pay homage to your client's expertise in one area while preparing her to accept information in another. I once told a client, "You forget more about engineering in these areas than I will learn in a lifetime, but let's look at the marketing side for a moment." Then I went on to talk about an area that I knew something about.

3. Find them a peer

If customers don't want to learn from you, bring along someone from your home office whom they consider a peer. Sometimes engineers like to learn from engineers, managers from managers, etc.

Application Question

Given my product area, what does my client need to learn to become more successful?

Motivating Your Customer by
Building Trust

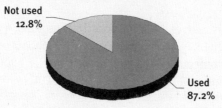

% of salespeople who have used this approach
in the past 12 months:

Not used
12.8%

Used
87.2%

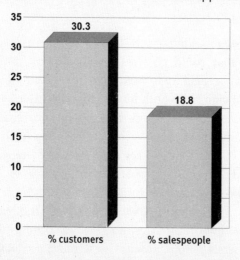

% of customers vs. % of salespeople
who think this is THE most influential approach

- 30.3 (% customers)
- 18.8 (% salespeople)

"Selling is a relationship, and what customers want most from that relationship is to be able to trust you and trust what you are telling them."

LEE IACOCCA, chairman and founder, EV Global Motors
(former CEO of Chrysler)

"Operating with integrity isn't easy because integrity only counts when it costs you."

GARY DAICHENDT, executive vice president,
Worldwide Operations, Cisco Systems

"Without risk, trust serves little purpose since not much is at stake. Risk generally stems from uncertainty about an important future outcome, or because one party is highly dependent on another."

from *The Trust Imperative*, by DOW, NAPOLITO, and PUSATERI,
published by the Strategic Account Management Association

When I began selling in the 1970s, I could anticipate most things that could go wrong with a sale. At the time prevailing thought held that trust was the result of a well-written contract signed by both buyer and seller. But in today's times of rapid change and ever more complex sales agreements, you just can't anticipate every variable. Where buyers once relied on a tight contract to protect their interests after the sale, today they need to trust the people they do business with. With uncertainty comes greater risk to the buyer.

Brian Tracy, in his book *Advanced Selling Strategies*, says trust is the most important sales function. According to Tracy, "Today customers are bombarded with so much conflicting and contradictory product information, the element of trust has become the indispensable ingredient in all sales relationships." Tracy contrasts the model of selling that existed before the 1970s—where the biggest part of the selling process, about 40 percent, was closing—with today's selling climate: "Today we have a new model that still has four elements in roughly the same proportion, but the elements have changed. In the new model the largest part of the selling process is building trust."

BRIAN TRACY'S OLD VERSUS NEW MODEL OF SELLING

The old model (pre-seventies)

The new model

40 percent: Closing

40 percent: Building trust

30 percent: Prospecting

30 percent: Identifying needs

20 percent: Qualifying

20 percent: Presenting solutions

10 percent: Establishing rapport

10 percent: Confirming and closing

Says Tracy, "Before the 1970s trust was not really a big part of the selling process, today it is the most important thing a salesperson does."

OLD THINKING Trust is based on a detailed contract between buyer and seller. If the details aren't worked out ahead of time and included in the contract, the deal is meaningless.

- -

WHAT'S DIFFERENT In times of rapid change sales agreements must be changed in mid flight. Also, consolidated buying and greater interdependence has increased the risk factor for the buyer.

- -

NEW THINKING As the risk factor increases for the buyer, buying from someone you trust becomes much more important. Without an underlying trust between buyer and seller, agreements are meaningless.

Approaches

ENGINEER "MOMENTS OF TRUST"

Typically, trust advances between buyer and seller in small steps over time and not in one dramatic meeting. Gerhard Gschwandtner, publisher of *Selling Power* magazine, calls these small steps "moments of trust." When I am working with an account I constantly look for things I can do that advance the level of trust the client puts in me. On the surface these look like small favors. When I achieve one of these moments of trust I think of it as winning a sale. I have worked for sales managers who, upon hearing of a small victory, ask me, "Great, Josh, but did you really sell anything?" I say, "Yes, I sold them the idea that they can trust me."

Typically, moments of trust come as the result of doing something special for a customer. This tells a customer that I am looking out for his or her interest beyond just the immediate sale. On a deeper emotional level, these actions tell a customer that he is more than just another transaction to me. If the customer is touched or impressed, I call that a win. When a customer thanks me for such a favor, I do not ask for one in return in the form of a sale. I know that once trust is established, far more will come back my way than I could win in a single sale.

Here are some things I have done for customers that created moments of trust:

Resolved a sticky billing dispute quickly and amicably

Helped find a new director of sales for a customer

Helped a customer find a hard-to-locate mailing list even though I don't sell mailing lists

Gave confidential career advice to a customer

Helped a struggling new company write a press release

These actions that created moments of trust may look like a list of small favors—and they were! But to the person I did them for, at the time that I did them, they meant a lot.

FOCUS ON LONG-TERM RELATIONSHIPS, NOT SHORT-TERM SALES

How often, when you contact a customer, is it to make a short-term sale? According to Anthony R. Gargano, president and CEO of AgileVision, "The very best account managers create a level of confidence in the customer so they always feel they are making the right decisions by taking their advice. These account executives take on a role that I call being a 'customer agent.' I have seen customers develop loyalty toward these individuals that is really incredible." Gargano's "customer agents" work hard for their customers and make trust building their top priority by being extremely knowledgeable and putting their customer's interest first time after time.

These "customer agents" are not company men who adhere

to every memo the home office sends. Says Gargano, "I've seen these account managers leave companies because they've felt they were being asked to represent something that was inconsistent with the kind of reputation they had carefully cultivated." Not surprisingly, they present a management challenge. Says Gargano, "Working with account executives who have this level of trust with a customer base means handling things a little bit differently. The first sale of a new product has to be internal. The account executives are the people who need to be sold first."

LINK YOUR INTERESTS

Robert J. Ritter, president of First Direct Corp., defines trust as "linked self-interest." Says Ritter, "I build trust by illustrating to a customer how my interests are linked to theirs. The moment they have a sense that your interests are linked to theirs, they say, 'Hey, I can trust him now.'"

Ritter describes how this works naturally between people: "Say you were to buy a product from a company where you were a close personal friend of the company president. Your friend the president assigns his best salesperson to handle your account. You don't know this salesperson, yet you're going to trust him because you have a long-term friendship with his boss that he does not want to hurt. So his interests and yours become linked. If he goofs up he will jeopardize his boss's friendship with you. On the upside he can make big points if he really takes care of you. Either way he has an interest in the outcome that goes beyond the sale."

That's how links happen spontaneously, but you can create them, too. Ritter suggests looking your customer in the eye, reminding her that you both work in a small industry or community, and saying, "If I don't deliver what I say I will deliver, word will get around, and my sales will suffer. On the other hand, if you are delighted with my performance, you will tell your friends and associates. My ultimate success is linked to yours."

There are more structured ways to pursue this strategy. Some sales organizations tie the salesperson's compensation to a customer evaluation program.

If you can convince your customer that your business success is linked to his success beyond any single sales transaction, he will have good reason to trust you.

BUILD TRUST WHEN THINGS GO WRONG

"The first time a problem comes up is a critical, defining moment in your relationship," says Gary Daichendt, executive vice president of worldwide operations, Cisco Systems. "Buyers and sellers are involved in much more complex arrangements today than ever before—partnerships, sole suppliers, electronically linked order systems, and multilevel sales functions—which means that the risk for the buyer has gone way up. The biggest concern of the buyer is, 'When things go wrong is the seller going to help bail me out?' "

When things do go wrong, Daichendt advises that you put relationships before contracts and pursue a dialogue: "A contract with a customer is good, but it's the spirit of the agreement that's more important. I don't want to get down to the line items of our agreement and start saying, well, we technically didn't tell them this or that. I tell myself wait a second, why did he or she buy from us? If it's reasonable to assume that we did imply this, then we have to live up to it. You have to get back to the reason you entered into the agreement."

Daichendt says that the integrity of the seller truly gets tested when problems arise. "Integrity counts when I've told you that this is what I intend to do and then find out later it's going to cost me more than what I thought it would. Now I'd better eat that expense because now is when it counts."

BUILD TRUST ON GIVE-AND-TAKE

When buyers speak of a salesperson they don't trust, they say, "He doesn't care about me, he just wants my money." It's easy to fall into this trap. As a salesperson, your job is to ask for the order and get business. But if every contact you make with a customer revolves around your need to make a sale, it's easy for the buyer to see you as entirely self-motivated. I try to start off every conversation with a customer by discussing something I'm doing for him.

A few years ago I started in a new territory in an industry where I didn't know anyone. Before I made significant contact with my customer base, I spent some time researching back issues of trade magazines and Web sites that covered the industry. Every month I would send a different mailing with another article about an interesting aspect of where the business might be going. Then, instead of starting my conversations by saying, "Hi, I'm Josh Gordon, I'm your new sales rep and I'm here to sell you stuff," I asked, "Did you get the article I sent you? Do you agree on where they say the industry is going?"

If you are calling on a group of people who all buy a particular product, service, or solution, they often have common interests or goals. I make a habit of collecting articles, funny e-mails, research studies, anecdotes, and success stories about the industry I work in. Items that you collect with one of your customers in mind can often be applied to many.

When I sold in an engineering field, I found that a lot of my customers were *Star Trek* fans. I started collecting articles and jokes about the subject. In another field, one of my customers told me his company was about to be taken over by a larger company. I found articles about what happens in these situations and sent them to him. I filed those articles for the next time this happened to one of my customers.

Whenever I'm planning to contact a customer I haven't spoken to in six months or so, I always send her something first.

The average cost of the product I now sell is about $5,000. When customers buy that from me, even though it's not their money, they feel like they're giving me something of tremendous value. On some level, they are asking themselves, "What has he done for me?" By consciously giving back to the customer, you'll dismiss that question from their minds. Customers who feel you are in a give-and-take relationship will trust you more.

TRUST COMES WHEN THE CUSTOMER COMES FIRST

Allen Jones, senior vice president, director of marketing, US Private Client Group, Merrill Lynch, has a simple formula for building trust. Says Jones, "Number one, put the client's interest first in everything you do, and number two, avoid even the appearance of anything inappropriate. Apply these two things to every circumstance and you will never go wrong."

If your company has several levels of customer contact at a major account, the issue of trust becomes important for all members of your sales team. If you have the trust of the operations director but not the purchasing agent, you won't make the sale. Remember that the purchasing agent and operations manager probably talk to one another. How do you send consistent messages?

Tom Moore, senior vice president of sales and general manager of the Fountain Division at Coca-Cola, proposes a simple solution. "When you're dealing with your customer at whatever level, just keep thinking, 'It's about them, not me.' It's so simple it almost sounds like a cliché. But in team selling situations, it's not as simple as it sounds. Every day different members of the team have to make different decisions and may not have the ability to coordinate with all other members of the team before proceeding. But if you corporately adopt the point of view that you are going to put the customer's interests first at all times, usually the right thing will happen and a high level of trust will be maintained throughout the organization."

Step-by-Step

1. MAKE SURE YOU UNDERSTAND YOUR CUSTOMER

Before you expect your customers to understand you, you have to understand them. And understanding requires an investment of time. Says Coca-Cola's Tom Moore, "There's a huge premium in today's environment on people's time. If you go to a customer and say, 'I'm going to invest two hours in an effort to understand where you're going,' those two hours will pay huge dividends down the road. If I am legitimately starting the sale, and the only destination in my mind is being able to truly understand my customer, then I'm going to be far more successful with that customer."

Customers that feel understood are more trusting.

2. TELL STORIES

Randy Schwantz, author of *The Wedge*, suggests that you can build trust by using stories to demonstrate your expertise. Says Schwantz, "A lot of sales people boastfully talk about their own expertise and what they can do for a customer. But when you visit a doctor, he doesn't come right out and tell you about his degrees and his diplomas and his credentials, he talks about how he may have treated a similar condition to the one you may be experiencing. He builds credibility by demonstrating his expertise as he talks you through a similar problem. It is the same thing when you are selling." Using stories to establish your own personal credibility is a great trust builder because you're not overtly selling yourself, you're indirectly selling yourself through a demonstration of expertise.

3. SAY SOMETHING NEGATIVE

Al Ries, chairman of Ries and Ries Focusing Consultants, suggests that the only way you can establish true credibility with a buyer is to share some negative comments about the buying situation you're in. Says Ries, "You can't just tell the truth when it helps. You have to sometimes tell the truth when it hurts. Otherwise, you might come off as being very lovable, but as phony as a three-dollar bill."

4. BE VULNERABLE FIRST

In larger sales both parties are at risk if things go wrong. As the seller, it is your job to be at risk first. "Your first action is to reach out to customers and literally put yourself in a position of vulnerability," says *Selling Power* magazine's Gerhard Gschwandtner. "Trust begets trust, and people judge you by your actions." Gschwandtner believes that if you feel comfortable in selling situations, you may not be going far enough. He says, "You need to be able to feel in your guts that the customer may take advantage of you. You may feel some paranoia and think, 'They're probably just pumping me for information, just shopping me, or may not return my phone calls after I submit a lengthy proposal.' Unless you have a feeling of vulnerability on an emotionally significant level, it doesn't count for the customer either."

5. BE CONSISTENT OVER TIME

According to Coca-Cola's Tom Moore, "Earning trust is a time-consuming process that advances when you deliver business results consistently over time. Without this consistency, you haven't earned a customer's trust."

One of the reasons that customers trust sellers is that they feel they can predict their behavior. This can come simply from spending time together. I have observed over the years that people who spend more time together trust one another more. If you have a customer who doesn't trust you, try spending more time with him or her. This may be easier said than done. If they don't trust you, why would they want to spend time with you? I recommend spending time together that is clearly identified as strictly social.

6. OFFER PROOF

I once made a sales call on a highly skeptical customer who'd had a bad experience with my company. I earned the right to make the presentation to him only after promising that I would make no statement I couldn't prove. During my call I made a lot of routine statements that are often taken at face value, but for this call, I documented everything. I backed even the simplest statement with a magazine article, a piece of research, or an anecdote from a reputable source. I am sure that most of the evidence I shared with him went unread, but it built trust when he realized that I was prepared to go out of my way to prove absolutely everything I said. Even when a customer doesn't ask for proof, you'll invite her trust when you take the time to provide support for what you say.

7. SELL REALITY

Scott Schiller, senior vice president, advertising and sponsorship sales at GO.com, manages Disney's online advertising sales force. In the Wild West world of Internet sales, Schiller adopts a down-to-earth approach: "The first thing we do is set realistic expectations. We don't sell anything or make representation of anything that isn't realistic. We do everything possible to achieve goals we set. It's easy to make bold promises when you are trying to get business. But sometimes the buyer isn't really looking for the best-sounding proposal, he's looking for the proposal that he trusts will play out realistically as time goes by. By cutting out the hype and selling reality, you'll build trust."

8. ESTABLISH COMMON GROUND

People trust what is familiar to them. Most experienced salespeople intuitively try to establish common ground for dialogue when they meet a new customer. Do you share the same interests, backgrounds, neighborhoods, or friends? The more you have in common with a customer, the more familiar you will seem to him. If people trust what is familiar, think about how you can become more familiar to your customers.

9. DON'T OVERDRESS

Whenever I visit a customer I try to dress at the same "level" as my customer. I have seen salespeople damage their relationships with customers by putting on airs and consistently dressing better than the customers they call on. I don't think this helps establish common ground or trust. On the other hand, there's no reason to dress significantly worse than your customer either.

10. CALL WHEN THERE IS NO SALE TO BE MADE

If you understand your product and the industry or group of people you sell it to, it's possible to look ahead and cultivate relationships with those who may soon be in need of your product. I once made a huge sale by proactively approaching a company that was not currently a customer of mine or any of my competitors. I approached them on the grounds that given the way technology was going, eventually they would be buying in my product area. I took the time to build a relationship with this company long before they were even considering buying what I had to offer or before they became familiar with any of my competitors. The years ticked by and they eventually became interested in what I had to sell. By that time I had a well-established trusting relationship. My competitors could not understand why they made so little progress with this account. The key was to build trust before there was an immediate sale to be made.

11. LISTEN MORE, TALK LESS

According to Brian Tracy, chairman and CEO of Brian Tracy International, in his book *Advanced Selling Strategies,* "Talking does not build trust, listening builds trust. There is no faster way for one person to gain the trust of another than by listening intently to what the other person has to say, and there is no faster way to undermine trust and irritate the prospect than by talking too much and listening too little."

Customers trust salespeople who listen carefully to what they have to say. They notice when you don't listen. Mike Massari, procurement manager at Videotek, told me, "If the salesperson is not taking notes, I don't think he's really listening to me. If there is no note taking, what that says to me is he's not taking what I have to say too seriously."

Coca-Cola's Tom Moore agrees, "Customers are savvy. They really know when you care about what they think. People know when you're listening. They can read it in your body language, they can see it in your eyes."

12. SAY, "I DON'T KNOW"

A pet peeve of Wheatstone president, Gary Snow, is salespeople who come off like they know it all. Says Snow, "A salesperson should know his product well, but he is not a designer or a strategic planner and I don't expect him to know everything. I respect the salesperson who is honest and tells me he doesn't know but gets right back with the answer I want. This builds trust."

13. IT'S ABOUT WHAT YOU DO, NOT WHAT YOU SAY

When I was about to graduate from college I thought I should buy a suit for job interviews. The salesman at the men's clothing store accurately sized me up as an easy mark. "Trust me," he said, "I am a very honest person and would never have you buy something you wouldn't like." Twenty minutes later I bought a suit that was 100 percent polyester ("easy care!"), dark chocolate brown ("did I hear you say you love chocolate?"), overlaid with a bright yellow grid pattern ("very stylish design"). I took his advice but I never wore the suit, and never went back to that clothing store. It has since gone out of business. I think most people have had a similar experience. Telling someone they should trust you often has just the opposite effect.

Reality Check

WHAT IF THEY JUST DON'T TRUST YOU?

The first thing to do is monitor your own behavior. According to Randy Schwantz, author of *The Wedge,* "The most common reason for buyers not to trust sellers is that their sales technique is showing. You never see the technique of the best salespeople. They have a very dialogue-oriented process." Wheatstone's Gary Snow adds that most salespeople routinely do things that undermine trust. Says Snow, "You don't trust someone who is trying to prove you wrong, or someone who debates with you. Yet a lot of salespeople do these things."

Second, don't assume that you have earned a customer's trust unless you really know that you have. Coca-Cola's Tom Moore says, "When you first meet a customer whom you have no relationship with, it's kind of like this: 'It's not that I don't trust you, but I don't trust you. You haven't demonstrated to me you're untrustworthy, but I have no reason to trust you either.' " Trust can never be assumed. It has to be earned.

Finally, consider what might be missing from the way you present yourself to a customer. According to Robert Guilford, a partner in The Trusted Advisor, "If you don't have reliability, you're a flake. If you don't have intimacy, you're a technician. If you don't have credibility, you're ill-informed, and therefore not trustworthy. And if you don't show enough interest in your customer's needs, you're just in it for yourself. If you are missing one of these dimensions it will have an obvious effect on your success."

If none of these is a problem then dig in for the long haul. There is no magic in the process. Just accept the fact that it takes longer to develop some people's trust than others.

WHAT IF THERE IS A TERRIBLE MISTAKE AND YOU HAVE LOST THEIR TRUST?

I once encountered a situation where a customer felt horribly betrayed by the organization I had just started working for. It took a long time to win back her trust. Here's how the time line went:

For the first two weeks the customer would not take my phone calls. I sat down and drafted a letter. I emphasized that I was the new representative and how I wanted to make things right.

As a result of the letter, the customer finally came to the phone. She gave me a good tongue-lashing about how disappointed she was with how things were handled. When I asked for an appointment, she declined.

For the next two months I dropped a couple of magazine articles and newsworthy items in the mail to her. After a while I was able to get her on the phone and arrange for a visit.

The first sales call was far from pleasant. Basically, I went in with a completely prepared presentation that never came out of my bag. She spent the entire meeting expressing how upset she still was. I thought a lot of this had been covered in earlier phone conversations, but I was wrong. I took out a notepad and took very detailed notes. I didn't respond to any of her concerns, but instead probed for more details on the problems she had experienced.

When I got back to my office I contacted my manager and we discussed her grievances line by line. We came up with a response to every one. I responded in writing to all of her concerns and repeated my responses in a phone conversation. In time we were able to move past the problems, but the first thing I sold her was the idea that she could trust me. Wheatstone's Gary Snow told me, "Some people are worthy of trust, and there are many customers who want to trust. If you are worthy of trust you can convey it." In this case it took a year.

Application Question

How can I help my customer feel that I and my company will "be there" for him when things go wrong?

4

Motivating Your Customer by
Selling Your Brand

% of salespeople who have used this approach
in the past 12 months:

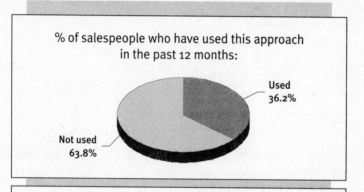

Used
36.2%

Not used
63.8%

% of salespeople using this approach vs. % of customers
who report being influenced by it in the last 12 months

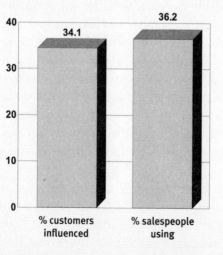

"The number-one tool our sales reps have is our brand. In my mind, our sales reps are brand managers."

TIM JOYCE, vice president, global sales, Nike

"When you're a big brand like MasterCard, everyone looks at you differently. At a bank, MasterCard is an acceptance mark; to the bank's customer, it's a credit card; to a magazine, we're an advertiser."

ROBIN BLUNT, vice president of Global Marketing Programs
at MasterCard

Fifteen years ago the sales manager I reported to herded our staff into the company conference room and proclaimed, "We are starting a new initiative to increase sales. We are going to sell our company's brand." I was given a color brochure with photos of happy, smartly dressed people in beautiful offices. The brochure copy made our modest company seem destined for greatness and I was commanded to begin every sales call by presenting this piece. The first client who laid eyes on it gave a loud, audible yawn midway through the second page. My next call yielded similar results and I stopped showing the brochure altogether. When the rest of the sales staff reported similar responses, our sales manager decided to find other ways to increase sales and left selling the company's brand to the marketing department—an arrangement that was more typical of those times.

Ten years ago there was little talk of the sales staff being actively involved in a company's brand management. Today, prevailing thought has changed dramatically. According to Ward Randall, managing partner of The Brand Consultancy, "When people heard the word 'brand' they used to just think in terms of advertising, logos, and public relations. In short, they thought of communications, and how a company communicated promises to its customers. But today, branding has another equally important dimension—delivering on those promises." Randall refers to this as "brand delivery" and says this involves every aspect of a business that touches customers.

At United Parcel Service, vice president of sales Joel Rossman describes how staff outside the public-relations department work on "brand delivery." "First off, every UPS truck is washed every morning before it leaves the garage. In addition, we work hard to train and motivate our sixty-thousand-plus delivery drivers so they develop relationships with customers and provide excellent service. Those drivers have an impact on why customers choose us."

With this shift in thinking to the dual focus on brand communication and brand delivery, companies have had to rethink how the sales force fits into brand management. Since the sales force is typically where a company makes and delivers on promises it now sits at the heart of a company's brand.

OLD THINKING	The sales force makes sales, the marketing team manages the brand.
WHAT'S DIFFERENT	Brand management isn't limited to communicating promises about what the brand can do. It's also about delivering on those promises.
NEW THINKING	If half the work of managing your brand is delivering on promises, then the sales staff has to be involved.

Approaches

BECOME A BRAND MANAGER

Every one of your customers has a slightly different perception of what your brand means. Your goal as part of the brand management team is to reinforce the positive, meaningful aspects of your brand—one customer at a time.

A customer formulates his perception of the value of your brand on a "what's in it for me?" basis. He wants to know what benefits buying a product with your brand on it offers him.

Benefits from brands can be economic or emotional. For example, if your brand is preferred by your client's consumers, it can spell increased sales to retailers. This is why local photo shops like to tell you they print on Kodak paper, card shops like to tell you they carry Hallmark cards, and computer makers tout that their computers have "Intel inside." That's an economic benefit.

When making a major sale, a brand's ability to communicate feelings of comfort and security to a diverse group of decision makers can often win the day. That's an emotional benefit.

Your job as a personal brand manager is to monitor your clients' changing needs—emotional and economic—and reinforce the benefits that come with buying your brand.

USE BRAND MOMENTUM

Gerhard Gschwandtner, publisher and editorial director of *Selling Power* magazine, recalls a customer motivation workshop that BMW did years ago. The plan was to teach the sales force techniques designed to uncover the buying motivations of customers. As they entered the automobile showroom salespeople were told to ask questions like, "Why look at a BMW?" or,

"Why do you want to look at this model versus that model?" The questions were open-ended and designed to answer the brand manager's question: What is it you expect from a BMW product that motivated you to come to this showroom today? When a customer walked into that showroom they had a positive expectation based on their exposure to the BMW brand. The salesperson's job was to take that momentum and move it forward.

If your brand is well managed and makes credible promises to potential customers, some of them will come to you with a predisposition to buy. You may field calls from potential customers you've never heard from before who seem familiar with your product. Often they're reacting favorably to your brand presence. When I get a call like this I ask, "What do you know about my product?" If the customer has a predisposition to buy based on a positive and accurate perception of my brand, my job is to reinforce it and quickly move the sale along.

Al Ries, of Ries and Ries Focusing Consultants, says, "Brands are much stronger today because people don't have the time to study various products before deciding what to buy. Life is complicated and the branding process simplifies it from the buyer's point of view. If I am buying a copier and buy a Xerox, how can I go wrong?"

BRING OUT YOUR CUSTOMER'S LATENT FEELINGS ABOUT BRANDS

I made a joint sales call with Paul Cohen, now director of hospitality and travel marketing at Enten & Associates, back when he managed sales for Harvey Research. We were visiting a client who kept badgering Cohen for a lower price. "But, Paul," said the determined client, "I can get this research study done a lot cheaper from Research America." Knowing that Research America (not their real name) was a low-priced, low-quality outfit, Cohen began a dialogue about company reputations by asking questions:

How would you describe the reputations of the different research companies who call on you?

How important is the reputation of the company you hire to do your research to *your* customers?

During the dialogue that followed Cohen skillfully brought out the customer's feelings toward these brands. Cohen well knew that Harvey's reputation was great and Research America's reputation was spotty. Then Paul looked the customer in the eye and said, "The thing you are not factoring into all of this is the importance of the Harvey brand." There was no more discussion of low-priced competitors. In fact, the customer bought on the spot.

When a customer's latent positive feelings about a brand are brought out in conversation, they become a powerful selling tool. Then you say "Okay, you feel this way about my brand. Others who are important to you—like your customers, distributors, partners, bank loan officers, board of directors, and your own sales staff—feel that way, too. Ignore them at your peril."

SELL THE IMPORTANCE OF BRANDS

I was once in a competitive selling situation where the product I was selling clearly had better brand recognition than its competitors. My skeptical client griped, "Okay, your brand is better than their brand. So what?" Instead of jumping into another round of us versus them, I sold against the deeper objection—this client did not believe that brands are all that important.

Anyone who has been to the business section of a bookstore

or who reads any business publication on marketing knows that brands are far more important in today's economy than ever before. Here are some ideas you can share with skeptical clients:

1. Brands are more powerful in the era of the Internet

Bill Etherington, senior vice president and group executive, sales and distribution, at IBM, says, "If you have tried to make any purchase on the Internet, the good news is that you have options, the bad news is that you have options. As you go on the Internet, we believe that brands have become even more powerful than before because the clutter there makes people seek value by looking for recognizable brand names."

2. Brands get the sale started faster in a more complex and busy world

If you talk to professional buyers you will find they have less time to devote to purchasing more and more complex products. Brands make the buying process easier. Says Marjorie Fagan, vice president operations media at Maier Advertising, "Brands are very important. If I'm buying ad space in a publication, it's important to me whether it's Intertec, Cahners, or Penton versus a publisher I've never heard of. When I see a promotional piece or get a phone call from someone I know at Cahners, that means something to me. Without that brand you are an unknown and you're really starting from the very beginning."

3. Brands future-proof a company

Will the supplier you buy from today be around tomorrow? If your customer buys from a company with a strong brand, the answer is probably yes. Companies with strong brands can take advantage of new selling situations. Says Scott Schiller, senior vice president of advertising and sponsorship sales at GO.com, "We have built up the Disney brand over the years and now along comes the Internet. Even though it's a new medium and things are being done differently, the Disney brand gives us an advantage. Right away people have expectations about us based on the brand, expectations that we build on and reinforce. We use this to build new relationships."

4. Brands are big business

I once sold the importance of brands by using a copy of *Ad Age,* a highlighter pen, and a helping of chutzpah. I bought a copy of *Ad Age* at the newsstand and highlighted every article about brands and branding. Then I marched into my customer's office, slapped the issue on his desk, and said, "I know you don't think that brands are important but let's look at who does." Managing a national brand is an incredibly complex and costly job that few people outside of the marketing business really see. Many of the articles in the magazine described the struggles of brand managers as they leverage their brands to launch new products or extend others. As my client started to realize just how much goes into managing a national brand, he saw that the subject of these articles was something important and that that "something" could be important to him as well.

SELL THE BRAND CALLED "YOU"

In a classic *Fast Company* magazine article called "The Brand Called You," Tom Peters wrote, "Starting today you are a brand. You're every bit as much a brand as Nike, Coke, Pepsi, or The Body Shop. To start thinking like your own brand manager, ask yourself the same question the brand managers at Nike, Coke, Pepsi, or The Body Shop ask themselves: What is it that my product or service does that makes it different?"

Says Bruce Himelstein, senior vice president of sales for North America at the Marriott Corporation, "When you make a call you are the brand. You are either adding or detracting to the equity of the brand every time you pick up the phone. We'd much rather you add to the equity by doing your homework, because once the customer picks up the phone, you are Marriott."

I once had a sales territory where I had to call on both TV production facilities and the manufacturers who made equipment for those facilities. Usually a television production facility is a very creative environment full of young, cool, highly imaginative people. By contrast, most of my equipment manufacturers came from engineering backgrounds and got really excited about making equipment that was, above all else, steady and reliable. There were days when at 10:00 A.M. I would be sitting across the desk from a client who dressed and acted like he worked at IBM, then find myself an hour later sitting on a futon with a client who dressed and acted like he worked at MTV. Much to the chagrin of my sales manager, I started wearing bow ties. Though slightly unconventional, it worked for both groups: My manufacturers thought I looked very *GQ* and my TV production facility customers thought I looked anti-establishment.

Step-by-Step

Telling a customer how great your brand is can sound like a lot of chest thumping and hot air. Selling your brand is a quality sell best done in a subtle way.

1. LISTEN DEEPLY FOR INITIAL BRAND PERCEPTIONS

Says Ward Randall of The Brand Consultancy, "When I say the word 'Kodak' to you, something happens in your head that you couldn't stop if you wanted to. There's a certain perception there. You may like it, or you may not, but you have a pretty clear idea of how it relates to you personally. This creates an expectation."

What kind of expectations does your brand create among your customers? Your brand has meaning to your customers whether it is intended or not, managed or not, and promoted or not. If you work for a company that does not have a brand management strategy, you may be selling what is referred to as an "accidental brand," a brand that develops on its own entirely based on customer reactions. I have sold under many accidental brands. To be successful, you need to be aware of the perceptions your brand has created in the market you sell to.

When I start a call where brand will be an issue I always ask, "What do you know about my company?" Then I listen deeply to the response. Sometimes it is not so much the content of the answer I listen to but its overall direction. If my customer describes the company as a leader or innovator, he may be impressed by leadership qualities. If my customer responds with a detailed technical rundown of the product line, it's possible that he is chiefly interested in the working details of how my product is created. If he mentions how others like or dislike the products my company makes, it is possible he evaluates a company or brand based on other people's impressions of it. The direction of the responses to your open-ended questions are real clues to understanding your customer's ways of evaluating brands.

According to Al Ries, of Ries and Ries Focusing Consultants, "In the past, salespeople would start calls assuming the customer was a blank slate. But salespeople now realize that prospects have strong perceptions about brands, and if they don't take the time to understand what they are, they're headed for trouble."

2. PRESENT YOUR BRAND

A. Sell Your Company

If your company has professional brand management a lot of your work is done for you. Says Bruce Himelstein, senior vice president of sales, in North America for Marriott, "If we are meeting with a new customer who is not familiar with Marriott, there are several communication vehicles we have to share. We have collateral pieces, videos, and portfolios. We have them for owner presentations, franchise presentations, and customer presentations."

Ann Belle Rosenberg, marketing manager for Video Systems, says that whenever she encounters an insecure client she pulls out a corporate profile of her parent company. Security can have more to do with the stability of your company and its ability to deliver after-sales service than it does with the actual product your customer buys. Says Rosenberg, "If you describe your company as reliable, and one that will be around for the long term, you can develop a feeling that your customer will be taken care of well after the sale is closed."

I often use a more personal, folksy approach. I position the company in terms of the customer-service people they have contact with. I try to know something about these people who are in contact with my customers after the sale. For example, I work with a terrific production coordinator to whom my customers speak regularly but few have met. A few years back, when she got married and changed her name, I made sure to tell all my customers. "Kathy has now changed her last name to Lewis," I would tell them. And I painted a picture of her in the most glowing terms.

B. Position your company

When you're selling a strong corporate brand, positioning your company positions the brand as well. Many buyers are skeptical when you attempt to position your company. They have seen too many overly optimistic, hyperbolic presentations. To do this credibly first remove the hype.

Start with your corporate brochure or annual report. Chances are good that your company's brochure says:

1. We are leaders in the field

2. We have the highest-quality products

3. We are focused on our customers

4. We are cutting edge

Guess what? Every other corporate brochure your customer has ever seen says the same things. Unless you are in a position to document all of the above with hard proof, keep it out of your presentation. In contrast, here is what you need to tell them:

1. Explain what your company does

2. Explain why your company is different

3. Explain what your company does best

4. Explain what your company does *not* do

The part I have always found buyers respond to best is number four—what you do *not* do. This part defines your focus.

C. Show him the media

A brand may live in the hearts and minds of customers but it is communicated through the media. Show customers your company's ads and articles. Says Tim Joyce, vice president of global sales at Nike, "Our sales force knows about all our media initiatives. They may not know what every TV spot will look like, but they will know what it's going to be about, and where it's going to air."

I once worked at a small company that received a favorable write-up in the local newspaper. I made copies for customers—most of whom would never have come across it otherwise. It was a big hit. An independent source confirmed in print everything I'd been saying about our products. You don't need a national media plan to make a lasting impression. When talking about an intangible such as a brand, showing can be more powerful than describing.

D. Use sophisticated brand research, but judiciously

With customers who are extremely sophisticated about marketing, it is possible to present your brand in quantifiable terms. Brand researchers can analyze subtle aspects of brands including their competitive presence, the preferences they generate in the market, and even how a brand will perform in forecasted situations. When I sold market research in New York City, I had a lot of these discussions. For most customers, though, this is overkill.

3. SELL THE EMOTIONAL BENEFITS

A. Brands can offer reassurance and security

Buying a brand product lowers the buyer's perception of risk. A company that has invested time to build a brand has a lot to lose by delivering shoddy products or services, and companies that invest the years it takes to build a brand are typically longer-term players.

B. Ask, "What is the feeling of your brand?"

Many company brands describe values that go beyond economic benefits. Some companies strive for community involvement, adherence to a cause, or advocate values.

Some might call Southwest Airlines a rate-cutting discounter. But Richard Sweet, senior director of marketing and sales for the company, describes that same fact in terms of the heart: "When we go into a city we want the fares to be low enough that a business person can expand their business to a new city because now he can afford to travel there on a frequent basis. We want families to visit families who they haven't been able to visit in the past because of the high cost of travel. And we want people to come back and fly with us over and over and over again."

Taking this higher road creates meaning that goes beyond the balance sheets. Says Guy Kawasaki, CEO of Garage.com, "Anything can be evangelized as long as it takes the moral high ground and makes people's lives better. It doesn't have to be hot, cool technology. You could evangelize salt if you had a special kind of salt that made people's lives better and you got excited about it."

C. Brands can appeal to pride

I once came home from a successful day of selling and was sharing the high points with my wife. That day I made two significant sales: a large sale to Greaves Corp., an industrial maker of electrical connectors, and a much smaller sale to a division of General Motors. Which do you think impressed my wife more?

How does your brand travel when your buyer goes home at the end of the day?

4. SELL THE ECONOMIC BENEFITS

A. Talk about "pull-through"

If your product has visibility to your customer's customers, the brand can have a very real economic impact.

Says Gregg Hammann, vice president of national accounts at

Coca-Cola, "Driving our brand meant first creating preference for our brand versus any other in the category. So if you walk down the street and you ask a consumer what beverage do you prefer drinking, we want them to say Coca-Cola Classic. Once we establish this, we talk to customers about using our brand to help promote their brand, whether it be for a restaurant chain or a grocery store. We tell them, 'Through the power of our brand working with your brand, we can bring more people in the door. So your business grows and our business grows.' "

Nike's vice president of global sales, Tim Joyce, says, "We spend a lot of time on what our brand means, and what it stands for. We ask, 'What is the brand going to stand for this season?' First we lay that down and the products follow underneath. We equip our staff to handle this by giving them planning tools so they can sit down with a customer and come up with an integrated marketing plan that charts the product flows for their customers."

Anytime your brand comes in contact with your customer's customers, you can make a case for the economic impact of your brand.

B. Use politics

I once almost lost a sale to a new buyer intent on making a name for himself. He came on the scene and started negotiating for lower rates very aggressively. I eventually was out of the running as he looked to off-brand products to drive costs down ever lower. For a year I lived without that company's business. Then through chance I met the president of the company at an industry function. When he found that his buyer was buying off-brand products and services, he became upset. He wanted his company to be perceived as world-class and not a bunch of bargain hunters. When he returned he reversed the buyer's decisions.

Brands enable people to make buying decisions when they are not intimately involved with the details of the products. I have seen a lot of top-down influence during buys based on a company president's perceptions of the company selling to him, or its brand. Sometimes top managers, eager to have their companies perceived as first tier, like to know that their organization has first-tier suppliers.

5. AVOID BRAND DAMAGE

Ward Randall of The Brand Consultancy explains brand damage this way: "Let's say you bought a roll of Kodak film. Based on your brand perceptions of Kodak, you expect the film to perform in a certain way. But what if it doesn't? That's brand damage. Brand damage occurs when the promises or expectations created by a brand are not delivered."

A. Your sale should be consistent with your brand

Your brand may imply a code of behavior. Selling in a style that is contrary to it can confuse brand perceptions. Several vice president sales directors told me that the days of the "Lone Ranger" salesperson are ending. One sales director told me, "If your entire sales staff is selling with approaches consistent with your brand but one guy is out there playing cowboy, that's a problem."

B. Don't sell the wrong customers

Says Tim Joyce, vice president of global sales at Nike, "We really try to get people to understand the positioning of our brand for the long term. Part of this means selling the right product to the right customer at the right time. No one has been fired at Nike for not hitting their sales goal. But we have fired salespeople for selling too much to the wrong customers."

C. Deliver on brand expectations during mix-ups

When a mix-up occurs with a customer, how do you settle it? Typically the paperwork gets pulled, fault is determined, and a concession is granted to the customer. The next time a mix-up occurs, put the formal agreements and contracts aside and ask, "Has our brand made any implied promises to this customer that we are not keeping?" Formal or not, adjust the concession to be consistent with the promise implied by your brand.

6. THINK LONG TERM

Al and Laura Ries wrote in their book *The 22 Immutable Laws of Branding,* "A brand is not built overnight. Success is measured in decades, not years."

As a salesperson, this is an important perspective. Ward Randall, managing partner at The Brand Consultancy, says, "Products have life cycles, but a well-managed brand can last much longer. Hundreds, perhaps thousands of products have come and gone under the Kodak brand. But the Kodak brand remains as viable today as it was seventy years ago."

Right now you have happy clients buying a product or service you sell. But in times of rapid change it is inevitable that this product will be modified, repositioned, replaced, or phased out. When it is time to sell them a replacement product or service, it is your brand that carries you through. I recommend selling beyond your product and taking some time to sell your brand. Think about your entire relationship with your customer. Now remove the product or service you sell. What meaningful things are left?

Reality Check

WHAT IF YOU WORK FOR ANNIE'S CLAY POT SHOP, NOT NIKE, SONY, OR MARRIOTT?

Selling your brand when you have a small company is often more important than when you have a big name behind you. Some extra points that apply:

1. Narrow your focus

Annie's Clay Pot Shop should never try to compete head-on with Home Depot. But Annie's can be the number-one brand if the arena it competes in is narrow enough. If Annie's claims to be the leading supplier of hand-painted clay pots in south Brooklyn, she can probably make her case.

2. Develop your own personal brand

I once sold ad space for a magazine that was not that different from its competitors in substance or quality. After a while I realized the path to success was to sell the "brand called me" first and the product second. When one advertiser rushed to place an ad during a week when I was on vacation, he called the home office and told them he wanted to place an ad in "Josh's magazine."

Application Question

How can I uncover, and monitor, the perception of my brand to my customer so I can clarify and reinforce the benefits that are meaningful?

5

Motivating Your Customer by
Building Loyalty

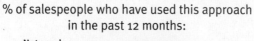

% of salespeople who have used this approach
in the past 12 months:

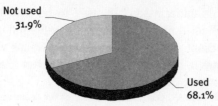

Not used
31.9%

Used
68.1%

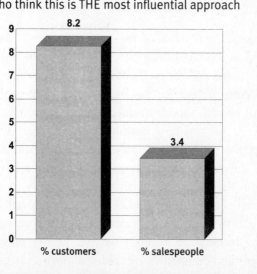

% of customers vs. salespeople
who think this is THE most influential approach

8.2

3.4

% customers   % salespeople

"In the future, a customer will go to your Web site, not like what they see, then click, and they're gone. A customer will go to your Web site, like what they see, but not the price, then click, and they're gone. A customer will buy something from you, have a problem that your customer-service people don't solve, then click, and they're gone, and you'll never get them back."

MARK JARVIS, senior vice president, worldwide marketing,
Oracle Corporation

"Client loyalty is under assault. It used to be that if you provided a high level of service you were assured that you would keep a client. But today, there are situations where somebody comes in behind you, develops a better relationship, and twists you out."

MARVIN FELDMAN, CLU, ChFC, president of The Feldman Group

Ten years ago most of my clients believed that customer service would differentiate them from their competitors and win customer loyalty. Today, customer service is every bit as important but the bar has been raised. National restaurant and retail chains have introduced every consumer to a better grade of service and now nothing less will do. If Toys "R" Us and Staples offer no-hassle, money-back policies, you'd better, too, and if excellent customer service isn't the standard in your industry or category yet, it will be soon.

As excellent customer service becomes a given, the way it relates to customer loyalty is changing. While customer service is still the foundation of any customer loyalty program, many salespeople and companies are taking a more strategic approach to loyalty that goes beyond customer service. They are developing customer retention strategies that build elements into their customer relationships to hold on to a customer's business.

OLD THINKING	If I offer excellent customer service my customers will be loyal to me.
WHAT'S DIFFERENT	In many markets excellent customer service is a given, so providing it is no guarantee your customers will remain loyal.
NEW THINKING	Loyalty is the result of engineering customer-specific strategies.

Approaches

BECOME INDISPENSABLE

David Fortanbary, director of cardiovascular marketing at Bristol-Myers Squibb, works with the sales organization that calls on doctors, encouraging them to prescribe their brand of pharmaceutical products. Says Fortanbary, "We have a mantra here that says we want to get into the DNA of the customer. That means without us they can't survive. To do this we work hard to make ourselves essential to our customers' core needs. The physicians we call on come to rely on us for the clinical and consultative support services that we provide."

On the consultative support side, Fortanbary's people provide a variety of information and services from business development programs to professional staff training in such areas as customer service. On the clinical side, Fortonbary's people have access to high-level scientific information to back up a doctor's expertise in any area. "Getting into the DNA of the customer" means working hard to become an essential resource for your customer's business.

Another great way to become indispensable is to get involved with your customer's customers. I once befriended an executive during a shared cab ride to the airport. During the lengthy trip we had a lively conversation and parted friends. He told me that he was the biggest customer of a client of mine. I found that keeping a relationship with my cab-ride friend had a very positive effect on business with my client. As long as I was friends with my client's biggest customer, my business was secure.

USE RELATIONSHIPS FOR DEFENSE

Often a relationship alone will hold business in place. A good relationship, regularly maintained, should give you an understanding of your clients' needs so you can initiate dialogue between your companies in changing times.

In addition, you should be using the relationship to defend your business. You simply have to find a way to monitor the perception of your own company's performance as well as your competition even if it seems unpleasant or out of place.

1. Ask for a performance review

Frank Coleman, vice president, AT&T accounts, at Lucent Technologies, has a question he likes his staff to ask their customers at least once a year: "What are we not doing that you expect us to do?" Says Coleman, "This is a key question that is not asked often enough. Many salespeople have in their minds what they are going to do for a customer the minute they meet her. Find the answer to this question first and then move on."

2. Monitor the competition

Joe, a sales colleague of mine, lost a huge account by forgetting he had competitors. Joe "bonded" with this client the day they met and as the years ticked by they became good friends. But an aggressive competitor was after Joe's business and began chipping away at this particular client. As Joe and his client enjoyed pleasant lunch after pleasant lunch, the competitor's name never came up. Joe's client was too embarrassed to bring it up with a friend and Joe just assumed the business was locked because of the good relationship. One day that competitor hit on an approach that caught the attention of the president of the company and Joe's good friend was told to go with a new plan. The friend had no choice but to drop Joe's business, telling him as he did, "I'm sorry Joe, it's business."

The irony is that Joe had an advantage he could have used. If he had known that his competitor was wooing his client, he might have used his established relationship and credibility to nip the threat in the bud.

Business friendships are my favorite part of the selling job but I never assume my customers are going to volunteer information about my competition or what exactly they may be offering. Making the relationship work to defend my business is my responsibility.

3. Work for one last chance before you need it

I once had a long-standing relationship with a great client who got terribly offended in a communication mix-up. He called me, upset, and canceled all his business with us. I could not believe how quickly the bad feelings escalated. I called my client to apologize and asked for a personal visit. But my client was so upset he refused to see anyone associated with my company. Because of my long-standing relationship, I was able to persuade my client to accept a visit, during which the misunderstanding was put behind us.

In a worst-case scenario, where an unanticipated event costs you the loyalty and trust of a good customer, a well-established relationship often gives you "one last chance." I have seen a lot of business saved this way. In these situations a well-maintained relationship is key.

SELL YOUR CORE COMPETENCY

There are a many things you can talk about during the precious face-to-face time you have with a client. You need to spend time selling your product or service but you also need to look to the future, when your product will be upgraded, modified, or replaced. Products come and go but the core competency of your organization is a constant, typically reflected in your products. Ask yourself, "What do we as an organization do better than anyone that is part and parcel of our products?" You can use the answer to sell and build loyalty. Do you offer:

The most universally used software in the market?

The machine parts made from the hardest steel?

The most-read magazines in the category?

The most widely accepted soft drink in restaurants?

Very often it is the deep values and core competencies of a company that result in these kinds of benefits. Spend some selling time talking about the importance of your organization's core competency and how it results in the basic benefits your customers like. Make sure your customer is a believer and you'll have steady orders even in changing times.

REWARD FREQUENT BUYERS

The mistake most companies make is to ignore their best customers in favor of chasing new ones. They forget about rewarding or thanking their best customers. Frequent-buyer rewards need not be expensive. You don't want customers wondering why you're giving them an expensive extra service they don't really need instead of better pricing.

Rewards can be personal in nature, like a nice dinner to say thank you. Often they are simply different ways of showing preference. Says Joe Uva, president of the Turner Entertainment Group, sales and marketing, "A lot of our customers in competitive industries are looking for an advantage. They like to get a first look at something new before it is offered to everyone. Within the context of best-partner relationships, we give our best customers a first look under the hood of the new offerings."

GET LOYAL CUSTOMERS TO TALK TO EACH OTHER

Herb Schiff, of Schiff & Associates, used to hold an annual dinner at an industry event for all his audio accounts. Since many people in this group were ferocious competitors who barely spoke to each other, the event was unique. Many looked forward to it. But Herb's real agenda was to get people who believed in his product to sit and talk to one another. One of the best ways to get loyal customers to stay loyal is to create an event where they can talk to each other and reinforce their feelings about your product peer to peer.

Step-by-Step

1. ASK YOURSELF, "HOW DIFFICULT IS IT FOR MY CUSTOMER TO SWITCH SUPPLIERS?"

Ground zero for any customer loyalty program is the cost, pain, or inconvenience your customer will incur if she switches suppliers. Will your client have to retrain a new group of people, will there be technical incompatibilities, will details slip through the cracks, will friendships be broken?

If switching from you to another supplier is completely pain-less, you have some thinking to do.

2. ASK YOURSELF, "WHAT WILL MY CUSTOMER LOSE IF THEY SWITCH SUPPLIERS?"

The answer to this question is buried in the specifics of your product and your customer's business. I have seen a number of businesses do special things for customers hoping to build in a unique element that cannot be duplicated elsewhere.

I know of a major trade show that has a point system for its exhibitors. The longer you exhibit, the more points you score and the better your booth location. If you drop out of the show—even for just one year—you lose all your points. I know of an exhibitor who wanted to drop out for a year but "stayed loyal" for fear of losing his accumulated points.

An ad agency once told an account I worked on that they had assembled the best group of minds anywhere in the industry to work on their account. The implication was that this team was irreplacable. The implication was also that if the client ever dropped this agency, this team could go elsewhere—possibly even to a competitor—with the same knowledge and skill set.

3. KEEP STEADY CONTACT

Good customers usually don't just get up and leave. Typi-cally, after their business is gone, someone will say, "We should have seen it coming." Frequent contact keeps small problems from escalating into catastrophic ones and helps good custom-ers become even better ones. The more often you contact a cus-tomer, the more loyal she will be. Marvin Feldman, president of The Feldman Group, takes that into account when it comes to his client base: "We try to have regular contact with all of our clients, even if it is nothing more than a phone call or a letter. It's imperative to provide that next level of service that lets the customer know 'I am here to service you, to help you whenever you need it.' "

4. MONITOR YOUR PRICING

According to research I conducted for this book, the number-one reason salespeople lose customers is that a competitor comes along and offers a lower price. In times of changing technology, improved methods of distribution, international outsourcing, and Internet services pricing, cost structures require ongoing competitive review.

While price alone is never the whole issue, a client who complains about your prices may indicate a weakness in your relationship that should be addressed.

For more on dealing with price issues, see chapter 17.

5. SET LONG-TERM GOALS TOGETHER

If you and a client set long-term goals together, he'll view your relationship as long term, too. Gregg Hammann, vice president of national accounts at Coca-Cola, says, "If you talk short term to customers, you put yourself in such a tight time frame that it can turn into a 'what have you done for me lately' conversation. We've had enough of those. Every customer is going to challenge you on an ongoing basis, but if you have a *long-term* strategy in place, even if you fail on a given tactic you can still get back in a favorable position with the customer."

6. START A LOYALTY BANK ACCOUNT

After you do something that builds goodwill with a client, you'll notice a change when you call on him. Goodwill pays off. When you show up for a sales call and the first thing that happens is that the client thanks you profusely for your help, that call is off to a good start. Conversely, when something goes wrong, a very different tone is set for future meetings.

I built up a lot of goodwill with one particular account and always had a very special feeling when I visited. Through an unfortunate set of misunderstandings, someone from my home office got into a screaming match with the president of this company. A week later we goofed up the production on one of their orders and a month later an important shipment arrived late. The feeling I had when I visited them next was anything but rosy. We worked through the incidents but the goodwill I spent years building had been "spent." My loyalty bank account was empty.

When I work on an account I always like to have some goodwill in my loyalty bank account to buy my way through the inevitable bumps along the road.

7. DOCUMENT WHAT HAVE YOU DONE FOR ME LATELY

Kevin Fitzgerald, editor in chief of *Purchasing* magazine, shared this story from a buyer: "For years a salesperson provided me with quarterly reports of the money that we were saving by buying from him. One day a new purchasing head came in and began tearing apart our supplier base. If there was no good reason why we were buying from a particular supplier and couldn't document value, the supplier was replaced by another one. I told this salesperson that had he not had that documentation of savings, he probably would have lost our business."

According to Fitzgerald, "Documentation is important for purchasers. Not only don't they have the time to do it for all the product lines they're buying, but sometimes they don't even know all the activities that a supplier is doing that are saving them money."

8. AFTER THE SALE...

As I close a sale the *next* sale is always on my mind. Some thoughts:

A. Excellent service is not an option today, it is a requirement

While sales organizations often reward salespeople lavishly for bringing in new business, retaining and building "old" business is often more profitable and grows a territory faster. Customer service is the selling you do to earn the next sale. Says Coca-Cola's Gregg Hammann, "Selling is not about pushing hard to get the sale and then relaxing on the beach somewhere. It's pushing hard to get the sale and then pushing even harder to make sure that you're following up and doing the things that you need to do to make sure it's successful."

B. Keep it simple

When you are structuring an agreement with a client, think about how this agreement will look the next time you come to them for repeat business. I find it is more profitable, in the long run, to give in on a few small points if it serves to make the overall agreement simpler. Agreements that are simple renew more easily.

C. Plan for mistakes

According to Frank Coleman, vice president, AT&T accounts at Lucent Technologies, "All suppliers have problems. To deal with them you need contingency plans. A contingency plan is like an insurance policy. When you fix a new problem, create a contingency plan for the next time that happens. If you get good at this you can make your contingency plans part of your value proposal."

Reality Check

WHAT IF YOUR CLIENTS JUST DON'T RETURN LOYALTY?

I once gave a client great service and did everything right, but was suddenly and inexplicably cut completely out of his business. After a year of extra-hard work I did get the client back. As we began doing business again I thought he might express some thanks for my extra-hard work that brought him back. Instead he told me, "Every few years I like to change around my suppliers. I like to cut them off and let them fight their way back in. Josh, it's not personal that I dropped you. But whenever I change suppliers everyone pays more attention to me, I get the best prices, and everything is great."

In conclusion: Sometimes loyalty is more about the nature of your customer than you or your behavior. Some customers will never develop a sense of loyalty no matter how hard you try. If you find you have one of these "never be loyal" customers, spend more time developing business elsewhere. Eventually you will lose this customer as he inevitably "changes around" suppliers.

Application Question

What are we doing today to keep an account's business if they went through a major reorganization, acquistion, or significant change in key personnel?

6

Motivating Your Customer by
Solving Problems

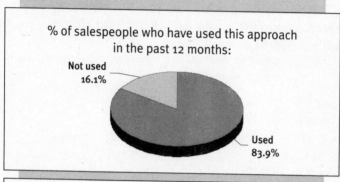

% of salespeople who have used this approach
in the past 12 months:

Not used
16.1%

Used
83.9%

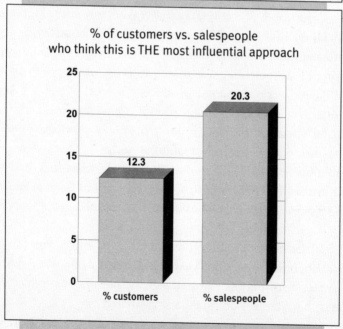

% of customers vs. salespeople
who think this is THE most influential approach

12.3

20.3

% customers

% salespeople

"When you solve a problem you're creating change. You have a status quo that is a problem and to solve the problem you have to change something."

DENNIS REKER, director of marketing operations for the Americas, Intel

"There is no 'selling.' There is no pushing your customer to buy. There's only the problem that you can solve for your customer. If you can't solve a problem for your customer, he will buy nothing from you."

CHRISTIAN TREMBLAY, president, Miranda Technologies

I knew in 1995 that selling had started to change when I visited the booth of a major computer company at the National Association of Broadcasters trade show. The booth was very impressive but it slowly dawned on me that something was missing here, something I had seen in every other booth I visited: There were no actual products for sale! When I asked about this a spunky, bemused booth attendant chuckled and said, "Oh, sir, of course we don't have any products to sell, we're just demonstrating capabilities today." There were no stand-alone products for sale at this booth; what they had to offer instead was the promise of customized bundles of products and services presented as "solutions" to problems that broadcasters were facing.

I left the booth thinking how unique and novel this "solutions" approach was. Four years later, at the same trade show, the majority of booths featured signage not about product offerings, but about "solutions" being offered.

OLD THINKING	Sell your core product; don't distract yourself or your customers by spending too much time on extra services or merchandising.
WHAT'S DIFFERENT	When a customer buys your product, she is often looking for a collection of services, information, and guarantees that work collectively with your product to solve her problems.
NEW THINKING	Don't sell products, sell solutions.

Approaches

TO SOLVE BIG PROBLEMS, SOLVE LITTLE ONES FIRST

I recently got a call from a client with a problem. He wanted to rent a specific database in my field that he couldn't find. I don't rent mailing lists, but I dropped everything I was doing for the next few minutes to tap into the resources of my company and find him a supplier. When I found one I went to their Web site, downloaded information my customer was looking for, and faxed it to him. Within two hours of his call he had the information he needed to solve his problem.

The solution to this customer's next problem may or may not involve him buying something from me. Either way, I'm going to help if I can because I'm building a reputation as someone on whom he can call with a problem and come away with a solution.

Says Christian Tremblay, president of Miranda Technologies, "In our industry you get problem-solving business through word of mouth. You probably get an invitation to solve a problem because you've done the right job for somebody else." But no one at Miranda rests on their laurels. Tremblay's sales group reacts quickly when these phone calls come. "We are paranoid. When we hear about a customer who has a new problem that we can solve, we race to solve it as fast as we can before someone else does. There is no internal pressure here on salespeople to respond quickly. The pressure we feel comes from the customer."

SELL YOUR PRODUCT AS A BUSINESS SOLUTION

When you present your product as a business solution you present it in terms of its ability to make an impact on your client's business. Often this means grouping products along with some know-how or service.

Let's say you sell cardboard boxes to moving companies. You could show up every month and ask, "How many boxes do you need this month?" But selling this way isn't making a business-level impact. You are just a supplier of a product that moving companies can buy from many competitors.

What if you showed up and said, "I am here to sell you a total containment solution. Instead of just selling boxes we can now provide all of the products needed to wrap or contain any object you are moving: tape, rope, bubble wrap, wrapping tissue, etc. In addition, for the next year we will track your orders on our new software and anticipate what products you are likely to need and in which months. From previous models we have developed, we anticipate that in the month of December in your area, there will be fewer moves but they will be from larger homes and offices. For this month you will likely need fewer supplies overall but more of our largest boxes. After a year we will give you a printout of what costs to expect for all of your moving-containment supplies so you can build them into your annual financial plan."

In short:

Don't sell cardboard boxes, sell a total containment-product program

Don't sell life insurance, sell an overall financial plan

Don't sell ad space, sell a marketing program

Don't sell a telephone, sell a business communication system

Are you providing a solution that has a business-level impact? Ask yourself this question: "How well does the chief financial officer of the company I am calling on know what I do for his company?" If your selling efforts have impact that goes beyond your buyer to the financial level you are being successful.

INITIATE SPECIFIC PROVEN SOLUTIONS

If you work out a solution that has an impact on a specific business situation, why not try and sell it to companies with similar problems? Sometimes the sell is easier because you can talk about the success you have had implementing the solution elsewhere. Joe Valenti, senior vice president at Xerox Business Services, has a sales team that focuses on this approach. They target companies that share common challenges and develop solutions to industry-specific problems. For example, Valenti's team has created a solution to help pharmaceutical companies control and speed up the massive documentation process of applying for Federal Drug Administration approval. Says Valenti, "If we can help a company accelerate bringing a drug to market by six months or a year, we can save that company millions of dollars."

UNCOVER LATENT PROBLEMS

Generally speaking, if your customer is aware of a business problem, she's already taken action to find a solution. The real magic of selling by solving problems comes from uncovering problems your customer didn't know she had. (More on this in the "Step-by-Step" section.)

PROBLEM SOLVING AT RFP TIME

There is no better feeling than when a client comes to you and says, "I have a problem, here it is, create a solution for me." The request implies trust in you as an individual and in your organization's capabilities. But when an RFP (request for proposal) is attached to it, it can be a different experience.

I was involved in one of these "call for solutions" for marketing services to help launch a new product. In reality, it was a cattle call of suppliers where the only "solution" being sought was a low bid for a predetermined package.

I had two choices: give them exactly what they were asking for and go for a low bid, or try to come up with a unique solution under restricted circumstances. Driven by my "idea guy" mentality, I went for the latter.

I started by asking the buyer in charge a lot of questions and found she had few answers. I asked if I could meet with the marketing VP to define the bid's objectives more clearly. She seemed annoyed at my request but agreed to set up a meeting. At the meeting I again started by asked a lot of questions. From what they were telling me, I realized that this product launch was going to flop. I told them that unless the product was re-configured for my market, they shouldn't waste their money on marketing services for a product that would never succeed. The RFP went into the wastebasket along with several of my competitors' bids. The client vanished from my market for a year. When they reappeared I was given an RFP with a wink and a nod that said, "Put in a bid that doesn't gouge us on price and it's yours."

When I have successfully problem-solved in the RFP process I have accomplished two things:

1. Got a meeting with the real decision makers

If I can't do this I forget about problem solving, turn in my best bid, and move on.

2. Redefine the RFP

If I get a meeting with the decision makers, I ignore the RFP, focus on the deeper problems and objectives, and try to find a better solution that redefines the RFP. I find that if I can help redefine the RFP, I almost always get the order.

PURSUE EARLY INVOLVEMENT

Conrad Coffield, vice president, broadcast and production sales, at Sony Broadcast & Professional Company advocates getting involved with problem solving while the problem is still being defined. Says Coffield, "Instead of getting involved after the client has made collective decisions on what they're going to do, we try to get involved before they have decided these things."

Coffield believes his group can offer valuable guidance at this early stage. He says, "We present ourselves as being able to really help this process along because we have helped others through similar situations. We understand what the driving business, emotional, and political issues are."

Coffield is quick to add that even when his company offers this free early guidance, there is no guarantee of winning the bid when the competitive RFPs go out. However, says Coffield,

"When we've spent a year working together in the early planning stages, there's a great deal of knowledge and trust that has been built that helps us when we send in our proposal."

Step-by-Step

If you hadn't noticed, the obvious problems your customers face have already been solved. The key to success is to be the first to uncover a latent or future problem and then present a solution. The challenge is to push the dialogue between you and your customers so that these issues emerge.

1. LEARN YOUR CUSTOMER'S BUSINESS MODEL

If selling a solution means presenting your product as one that will have an economic level impact, then understanding how your customer's business runs is essential. Says John Kinnaird, vice president and general manager, Preferred Account Division, at Dell Computer, "I don't want my salespeople just selling boxes, I want them selling solutions. Since we call on people who run businesses, we teach our salespeople how to run a business. They have to know what a profit-and-loss statement is and how hard it is to hire and keep good people. We give our salespeople a month of training a year. They get it in off-hours, on weekends, and before or after work. We also provide audiotapes and online training."

Whenever I take on a new product to sell, I always ask, "How do the people I am calling on make their money?" In today's economy, that's not always obvious.

I had always assumed that a small software company I called on made its money by selling software packages. I was wrong. One day the president of the company explained that he barely breaks even selling software to his customer base. He makes his money selling software upgrades. When I adjusted my problem-solving conversations to include this, I was more successful.

2. BECOME KNOWN IN YOUR MARKET AS AN EXPERT

One way to motivate customers to come to you with their problems is to earn a reputation as an expert. If you can accomplish this, customers will find you. Says Paul Werthman, western regional director at Framatome Connectors, USA, "We're a very low-tech company, but we have a very high-tech engineering side. When we demonstrate how we can take this low-tech product to another level, it's very impressive. Once customers see this they realize that we are the experts, and they send their questions and their business to us."

3. SET UP A PROBLEM-SOLVING SESSION

If your customers are not calling you to problem-solve then it's time to call them. I find opportunities to suggest problem-solving sessions on routine sales calls. I notice an area of their business where we have helped others in the past and say, "We have helped a lot of clients be more successful in this area. If you like, we can set up a visit to explore how we can help." I might also share some nonconfidential information to back up my claim.

If the project looks substantial in size or scope, you may want to ask your client to have others at the meeting as well. I find I can usually get a client's higher-ups or people with higher-level expertise to the meeting by offering to bring their peers in from my organization.

Sometimes the solution to a problem becomes obvious when the right people sit down to examine it. Your job is to act as the catalyst behind the meeting.

4. GET THE DIALOGUE STARTED

A. Look to the future

If your customers do not think they have any problems at present, Marvin Feldman, president of The Feldman Group, advises them to look ahead. Says Feldman, "If I only take care of today's problems when I meet with a client, as soon as I walk out the door everything I've done is out-of-date. My job is to understand my customers and their situations to the point where I can work with them to prevent problems that might be coming a few years out."

Many buyers don't like talking about problems because it can reflect badly on them. No manager wants word to get around that his department has a lot of "problems." When you shift the dialogue to focus on the future, their defensive posture goes away. Instead of your client looking like a poor manager whose department is besieged with "problems," he looks like a proactive leader anticipating the future.

B. Help your customers cope with change

One of the biggest "problems" any client faces today is that of successfully dealing with change. I often refer to "industry-wide change" to initiate problem-solving dialogues. I find that if I can share meaningful, nonconfidential information on how other companies are coping with change, I usually get customers' attention. It is important to be able to put something substantive on the table and not just casually chat about it. I use case studies, "best practices" stories, and research on trends.

Says Dennis Reker, Intel's director of marketing operations for the Americas, "At Intel, we have a saying that change is our ally. If you're not changing things or helping people change things, then somebody else is going to change it for you. Like the old saying goes, if you're not the lead dog, the scenery never changes."

5. KEEP THE CONVERSATION GOING

If a problem-solving session becomes mired in abstract ideas, it's not going anywhere. Your job is to refocus the conversation and keep it going. I once had a meeting that continued for over an hour without any solutions in sight. But by keeping the conversation focused and moving, we eventually developed several viable solutions. When it was over the client turned to me and said, "I really didn't think we were going anywhere for a while but I am glad we stuck it out." Sometimes the initial stages of a problem-solving meeting serve only to make people comfortable with one another and used to the idea of working together. I have seen meetings where nothing of substance was discussed for the first twenty minutes as people in the room postured and felt each other out. It's hard to rush this process but you can keep it moving forward.

6. HELP YOUR CUSTOMER DEFINE HIS PROBLEM

Says Chris Leibfreid, managing director of the CRM Group, at PricewaterhouseCoopers, "Sometimes you come across a customer who has a problem but doesn't know the cause. For example, a company that is losing customers for no clear reason." Leibfreid recommends asking a lot of questions and listening hard to the responses. He says, "What we pride ourselves on is being able to listen to the customer, understand what the problem is, and then propose some kind of a mechanism, whether it be a technology solution, a change in process, or a change in organization, to address the problem."

I always look for a moment in the conversation where the client looks up and says, "You know what would be really great? What if we could . . ."

At that point you move from nailing down the parameters of the problem to nailing down the parameters of the solution.

7. ASK ABOUT THE SOLUTION

Robert Guilford, partner at The Trusted Advisor, has a unique approach. He asks the client, "What would it look like if we solved this problem?" Guilford then hands his client a sheet of drawing paper and a pencil. He adds, "Why do consultants immediately jump up to a flip chart and diagram out what is under discussion? They do it because it helps focus the issue and illustrate it in a way where solutions present themselves. Your client will not necessarily draw you an artist's picture but it may help him see his problems in a whole new way."

Reality Check

WHAT IF YOUR CUSTOMERS DON'T HAVE ANY "PROBLEMS"?

Some customers resist talking about problems or deny having any. If they were the ones who bought the products or services now in use, then admitting to problems is like saying they made bad decisions. Randy Schwantz, author of *The Wedge,* advises against pushing customers too hard if they don't want to talk about their problems. Instead, he suggests, "It's easier to get someone to admit what they have is not perfect than to get them to admit they have a problem. Ask questions and get him talking about his current situation and its shortcomings. Ask him how it could be improved. Then compare what he has with what you can offer."

Some things that you might think of as "problem solving for customers" are not viewed as such by customers. During the time I was writing this chapter, I bought a new suit. I tried on a European suit and some funky styles that I never seriously considered purchasing before I settled on a suit I really liked. I had fun! I think of buying a new suit as a treat, not as "solving a problem." Don't get hung up on the words. If your customer doesn't want to talk about "problems" you can still have a productive conversation.

Frank Coleman, vice president of AT&T accounts at Lucent Technologies, suggests that you can overcome resistance to talking about "problems" by broaching the subject in a different way. Says Coleman, "If your customer doesn't want to talk about a problem, instead you might talk about a strategic objective that they have to obtain, a better way they can serve their customers, how they can operate more effectively, or how they can differentiate themselves in their markets."

Application Question

How can I package my products together so they solve a business level problem for the companies I call on?

7

Motivating Your Customer by
Sharing Ideas

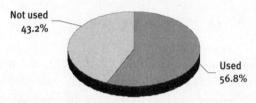

% of salespeople who have used this approach in the past 12 months:

Not used
43.2%

Used
56.8%

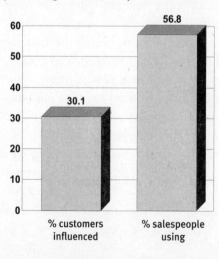

% of salespeople using this approach vs. % of customers who report being influenced by it in the last 12 months

56.8

30.1

% customers
influenced

% salespeople
using

"The better an idea, the more it will threaten people and the less accepted it will be."

GUY KAWASAKI, CEO of Garage.com and author of *Selling the Dream*

"We are merchants of change. We thrive on driving change into the marketplace. In many cases, companies are resistant to change because it's hard and disruptive."

FRANK PINTO, vice president, worldwide sales, Sun Microsystems

I have always been an "idea guy." When I started out selling in the early 1980s, many of my customers viewed this as a curiosity. While selling in the less volatile business climate of that time, my clients viewed my idea-generating talent largely as a form of entertainment. As my ideas led us to various "what if" scenarios, most of my clients were thinking, "Hey this is interesting but it isn't really going to happen to me or my company. It's not really about me!"

But today, successful companies recognize that change is inevitable and finding good ideas to help keep pace with it is a priority. Ideas have emerged as a new currency between buyer and seller that can literally be worth more than money.

I once shared an idea for a new product with a client who went on to develop it into one of his company's most successful products. Likewise, insightful customers willing to share new product ideas can be among a company's most valuable assets. Kevin Kelly, in his book *New Rules for the New Economy*, says that good products and services are cocreated between buyers and sellers. Kelly concludes, "Whoever has the smartest customers wins."

As an outsider visiting clients who are all looking for solutions to similar problems, you are exposed to a variety of ideas about their business. This gives you a valuable overview of your customers' field that no individual company has. You can use this outsider's perspective to your advantage—and to theirs. I have totally "wowed" clients with ideas gained simply through my own outsider's perspective. The key is to look actively for nonconfidential ideas that you can use to build your own "idea currency."

Many decision makers hide behind intermediaries who are buyers in name only. I often use my idea currency to get past these gatekeepers and into the big office. As one general manager told me, "Getting ideas is the only reason I meet with salespeople. I can get my prices off a rate sheet and product information from your Web site. If you don't have ideas to share, I can do my buying without you."

OLD THINKING	Customers like hearing new ideas but resistance to change means resistance to ideas.
WHAT'S DIFFERENT	In an environment where your customers are forced to change just to keep pace with their competition, new ideas are welcome.
NEW THINKING	Ideas have acquired new value in our fast-changing world. They represent a new currency for salespeople that can be more valuable than money.

Approaches

In the typical Hollywood business movie, the hero walks into the boardroom and forcefully presents a bold, revolutionary idea. A few sound bites later the room is full of stunned executives seeing the light. "Why didn't we think of this before?" gasps a grateful CEO as the movie's story line veers sharply toward a happy ending. I sell with ideas every day, but there is never high drama like this. Selling with ideas is more about hard work than blinding creativity, and more about working a dialogue with your customers than overpowering them with a presentation.

START AN IDEA DIALOGUE

Many of the great selling ideas I use were cocreated with clients on routine sales calls. I know my products, my company's value-added programs, and how flexible we can be. My client knows what his company's budget and needs are. Working together, we can generate ideas that make profit for his company and more business for me. You have the power to turn a sales call into an idea-generating session. Here's how to do it:

Before you go on a call, try to learn everything you can about a client. Visit their Web site. Think about what you have learned about them in the past. Then think about what ideas you can bring to the table to get things started. These initial ideas are critical because they will either start a dialogue or kill it. As I brainstorm ideas before a meeting I remind myself that:

- A selling idea is about their business, not my products

- A selling idea must be about something new

- A selling idea must benefit them

Your goal is not to come up with *the* idea, but rather to come up with several ideas that will start a dialogue and get the client thinking about new possibilities that involve your product.

I once called on a tough client who up to that time had given me very little business. I got the appointment with difficulty and only after telling him that I had some great new ideas to discuss. After he reluctantly agreed, I racked my brain for a week to come up with some. I asked everyone in my company for help. On the day of my appointment I had six ideas typed up, preapproved, and ready for presentation. He showed up twenty-five minutes late for our appointment and, without an apology, started the meeting by saying, "So, what have you got?" I went through my ideas one by one. He dismissed the one that I thought was a standout as ordinary. But another that I thought was routine dazzled him. "Wow, this is brilliant," he exclaimed as he stood up from his desk and asked if he could copy that page of my notes. Before I could explain that I was going to leave him a copy of the entire presentation, he darted out of the room, page in hand. Moments later he returned with a different attitude toward me and my ideas. Finally I had a better understanding of what ideas got him excited. It was the dialogue resulting from a variety of shared ideas that broke the ice, not coming up with one big killer idea.

START AN IDEA CLIP FILE

Chris Leibfreid, managing director of the Pricewaterhouse-Coopers CRM Group, says that it's important to be able to recognize situations that would benefit from a service or product you already provide. Says Leibfreid, "We start by asking questions, but if we hear something that sounds familiar, we might ask questions that steer the conversation toward an area where we have some experience. After all, if you see hoofprints, don't think rabbit, think horse." But Leibfreid cautions that if you jump to conclusions too quickly you can miss opportunities as well.

The idea need not be revolutionary. In sales, a "new idea" is simply an idea that's new to your customer. Collect nonproprietary ideas you come across in your dealings with customers and share them with other customers. Most salespeople I know just keep these ideas in their heads. I know one salesperson who keeps them in a special notebook, and a sales organization that has its salespeople formally log them into their company's intranet. I have two file drawers stuffed full of them.

SELL THE IDEA BEHIND YOUR PRODUCT FIRST

Lyn Brigham, eastern sales manager for American Flexible Conduit (AFC), sells metal-clad electric power cable. While her product significantly reduces her clients' expenses, it also replaces the traditional "pipe and wire" process that electrical contractors have used for many years. Sometimes it's a tough sell, but Brigham knows that if an electrical contractor buys the idea of metal-clad cable from her, he will likely buy the cable from her as well.

Selling the idea first can help you avoid an adversarial relationship with a buyer. If you simply present a product for purchase and attempt to overcome all objections, the buyer may not feel emotionally ready to buy. And if she is not ready to buy, she is going to work extra hard to come up with more objections—behavior you do not want to encourage.

Presenting the idea first means making the sale in two steps: first the idea, then the product. The customer who buys the first step isn't making a commitment, but the process keeps the sale moving forward and prepares the customer emotionally for the actual buy.

Presenting an idea first lowers the risk for the seller as well. If your customer rejects your product, coming back is tough. But if your client rejects an idea, you can just come back with another selling idea.

DEVELOP A "THOUGHT LEADERSHIP PIECE"

For Mike Peters, director of sales and marketing for the Americas at PricewaterhouseCoopers, presenting an idea in the form of a "Thought Leadership Piece" is a key to success. Says Peters, "We develop a thought leadership piece where we describe an idea or a process for improvement and publicly share it. This sharing can be in a book, a white paper, a section on a Web site, a seminar series, or a speech. What this does is make us known as a group who owns a particular idea or area of interest in the business community. A potential customer might see this and say, 'I think we could use this but we want some help. Now, whom should we ask for that help?' " Peters hopes they call his company.

Using thought leadership pieces need not be as elaborate as putting on a seminar series or writing a book. I once did a series of mailings to my advertiser clients encouraging them to view their trade advertising as an investment in their companies' brand. Every two weeks for a period of two months I copied an article on the subject of branding through trade advertising and mailed it to my clients. In a small way I became the thought leader on the subject as several of my customers sought me out when they needed to know more about the subject of trade advertising as a brand-building tool.

Come up with an idea and share it with as many people as you can for free. If people are intrigued by your idea, they will come to you asking for help and bring business your way.

Step-by-Step

When you sell an idea, you are asking an individual or organization to accept change, a difficult thing to do. Here's how to present the idea in a way that improves the chances that it will be accepted:

1. FIRST, FIND THE IDEAS

A. Be open to something new

According to Gerhard Gschwandtner, publisher and editorial director of *Selling Power* magazine, "Ideas are always there. They are in the customer's mind. Bits and pieces of ideas are always floating around you and are inherent in every selling situation. You need to be open to discovering something new. If you have the right attitude and are open to discovering ideas, you will draw them like a magnet."

B. See through your customer's eyes

My favorite way to generate ideas is to try and see the world through my customer's eyes. I first try very hard to establish a working understanding of my customer's needs and goals, both on a personal and professional level. I take notes on every call for later reference. As I go about my daily routine I try to hold on to these impressions. In the course of my day I often notice things that would benefit my client.

Early one morning I was out jogging on the streets of Brooklyn when I took a turn down an unfamiliar side street. The street was run-down and I was glad to be speeding through. Halfway down the block I caught a glimpse of a badly faded sign with a familiar name on an abandoned building. I backtracked to find a battered sign with the name of a large industrial client of mine that had since moved to much larger offices in Connecticut. I realized that my huge corporate client started their business in this tiny, unassuming building.

Remembering that this was a company that prided itself on its history, a selling idea began to form. A new vice president whom I wanted to impress had started two weeks earlier. I went back to the building the next day and took some photographs. Then I bought a do-it-yourself-award-plaque kit at an office-supply store and assembled an award-style plaque showing the modest building. On the plaque I laser-printed, "As you begin your challenges at this new company, remember: From humble beginnings can come greatness." The plaque was a huge hit. It got me in good with the new VP and the plaque hung in his office for years afterward.

C. Talk to your customer's customers

According to Jim Wattenmaker of Wattenmaker Advertising, "Very often the person who buys from you is not the person who uses what you sell. The best way to talk to your customer is to talk to your customer's customers first. It's one thing to come up with an idea that is clever that stresses a quality of your product, but if it isn't meaningful to the end user, it won't get high marks. Ideas that are really meaningful come from digging into what the ultimate customer is doing, selling, buying, or wanting."

D. Follow changes in your customer base

The career of Lee Iacocca is synonymous with great ideas: the Mustang, the mini-van, and now the E-bike. But these innovations were not the result of random ideas that just popped up. According to Iacocca, a self-confessed "research nut," they came from following changes in his target customer, the baby-boom generation. Says Iacocca, "We came out with the Mustang when the baby boomers were teenagers who were looking for a sportier form of transportation. Years later those baby boomers had a couple of kids, a dog and a cat, and they needed utility so we developed the mini-van. Now those boomers have grown kids, and I'm going to deliver an electric bike so they can have fun, and be fit into their retirement." Iacocca's formula for coming up with great ideas is to love your customers, get to know what they are doing with their lives, and ask yourself, "What do my customers need today that's different?"

E. Subscribe to the trade magazine your customers read

I once started a new sales territory by asking my clients which trade magazines they read. They all mentioned a magazine that had a subscription price of over one hundred dollars a year. My shortsighted employer would not allow me to put a subscription on my expense account, so I paid for the subscription myself and had it mailed to my home address. Soon I was selling accounts that my employer had never heard of and was coming up with selling ideas that no one else had thought of. Everyone thought I was a creative genius but the truth was that many of my new ideas and sales leads came directly from that magazine. I never told anyone how I did it, but instead deferred to the words of Albert Einstein, who once said, "The secret to creativity is knowing how to hide your sources."

F. Steal 'em

Sid Friedman, president of Corporate Financial Services, has a reputation for regularly wowing his clients with clever ideas. Says Friedman of his ideas, "Every one is stolen, stolen from wonderful people, all over the world." Even Friedman's wife is not immune. According to Friedman, "I've been sending out birthday cards to my clients for thirty-five years with little response. On my fiftieth birthday I got a special card from my wife. It was a pop-up card with a Disney character on it." Friedman stole that idea and now sends out these cards to his clients. He reports, "I used to send out birthday cards and my customers would throw them away. But when I started mailing these cards, people called me up and said, 'Sid, this card is fabulous, where did you get it?' "

G. Believe in your ideas

To sell an idea you have to believe in it. Today, a lot of people listen to the ideas of Ted Turner, now vice chairman of Time Warner Inc., but it was not always so. Back in 1970 Turner used profits from his father's billboard advertising company to buy a financially troubled independent UHF-TV station. Through innovative thinking and believing in his ideas he built that station into a media empire. When asked how he can be so convincing Turner replied, "My personal motivations usually come from a real belief that anything is doable. I believed in cable television from day one. I also believed in a twenty-four hour news channel from the very beginning, because people like to learn, to be educated, to be challenged."

2. SET UP THE APPOINTMENT WITH SUSPENSE

There's a great temptation to completely surprise your customer when you unveil your brilliant idea, but you'll rarely make a sale that way. Often your customer needs to enlist the support of other people in the company or needs to prepare herself so she can intelligently respond to it. You have to pre-sell the idea without giving it all away. If you give the idea away completely, your client may feel she can evaluate it on her own without wasting time in a meeting. You need to share just enough to generate interest but hold back on the details until you can present them in person.

3. ASK FOR "IDEA AMNESTY"

When you present an idea to a client who must decide to buy it or not, there is judgment in the air. Ideas do not develop well in this environment. I have successfully presented ideas by asking for a suspension of judgment. I explain that what I'd like to do is some brainstorming. At a brainstorming session people free-associate and are encouraged to come up with ideas even if they sound crazy or impractical. During the session there is no judgment made on any ideas and the goal is to generate as many ideas as possible. The sorting-out comes later. This initially allows all kinds of ideas to float free, be combined with other ideas, or potentially develop into more useful ideas.

If your client is open to new ideas and believes that suspending judgment will help come up with better ideas, he may go along with you. Says Larry Wilson, author of *Stop Selling, Start Partnering,* "If you always do what you've always done, you'll always get what you've always gotten. And you'll always do what you've always done if you always think like you've always thought." Larry suggests that the way to improve performance and results is to be open to thinking differently.

4. PLAY THE UNDERDOG

Selling a new idea can make you feel like the new kid in town who has to prove himself. Sometimes this situation can work to your advantage. Says Karen Lukanovich, president of Simon River Sports, "There's something in human nature that makes people want to help out the underdog. People will usually give you a chance if you hang in there long enough because they like to give the underdog a shot. Often underdogs are the ones that have a more humble approach."

Adds AFC's Lyn Brigham, "Sometimes I get more time out of someone who doesn't like my ideas than someone who does. People who don't like my new idea usually think they know it all and want to get their two cents in."

5. PUT THE IDEA ON A STAGE

Sometimes reacting to an idea requires more thinking than a client wants to engage in. But if your client doesn't react to your ideas you have gained nothing. I find that if I call attention to the idea, and describe it as something important, and ask for a response, even the laziest clients will respond in some way.

During informal idea sharing I put the idea up on a stage by saying, "I have an idea for you." Then I pause a beat before going on. This establishes that I am verbally presenting something for consideration. In a larger, more formal presentation, I do the same but on a grander scale. I might describe how much work went into developing the idea before presenting it or share some history about how the idea was developed.

6. PRESENT THE IDEA WITHOUT INTERRUPTION

You will present an idea more powerfully if you have the chance to state it completely without interruption. If you stop and address even well-intentioned questions, often the full power of your idea will get lost. I say, "That's a good question and I am glad you asked it. But this question and others like it will be answered as I explain my idea further. I will be glad to answer any questions later but give me a chance to explain the whole concept first."

7. THE FIRST FIVE MINUTES

The first five minutes after you present an idea for the first time are the most critical in the sale. If your audience decides it lacks merit, it will be dismissed after a short polite discussion and the meeting will roll on to the next subject. If the idea is deemed worthy of consideration, you'll explore it in greater depth together. After an idea is presented for the first time there are usually objections raised that can sweep it off the agenda and into oblivion. I always rack my brain to anticipate these initial objections. If you can survive the first five minutes you're on your way.

8. PURSUE AN ADAPTIVE DIALOGUE

It is presumptuous to think you know enough about your customer's business to present an idea that would be adopted without some kind of modification. Usually the only way to sell ideas is to adapt them to your client's specific requirements. In the process of the dialogue that follows, your job is to keep the idea moving along. Let go of any defensive feelings should the idea be significantly altered from its original form.

9. TO CLOSE THE SALE, GIVE THE IDEA AWAY

Anytime a customer offers slight modification of the idea, make sure you give the ownership of that modification to the person. If a buyer feels ownership in an idea he may become its advocate and fight to see it implemented. Over the course of the meeting your job is to give the idea away to a champion at the company that you hope to sell. Ideas that no one "owns" often fade from the company's agenda. Without an internal advocate, most ideas simply are forgotten the minute you walk out the door.

10. HOLD ON TO THE SALE AFTER YOU'VE GIVEN THE IDEA AWAY

Part of the risk of selling with ideas is that after you share the idea and give it away, a customer can take your idea and then go buy the product needed for its implementation from your competitor for 5 percent less. The challenge is to sell your expertise along with the idea. When you sell your idea, make sure your customer is convinced that you are an integral part of the package. AFC's Lyn Brigham's customers think of her as someone who sells the idea of using metal-clad cable, but also as someone who can help them use the product better once they have bought it.

11. IF IT DOESN'T STICK, GO BACK AGAIN

If you don't make the sale, prepare for the next time. Sometimes your client's decision to buy or not buy has more to do with internal issues at his own company than with how well you presented the idea. I once represented the same program (slightly repackaged) three years in a row. The first year potential customers found the proposal interesting, the second year they got used to the idea, and the third year they bought.

Says Brigham, "Even if I don't make the sale, my customer smiles and I smile and I leave knowing that he still likes me. I leave on a friendly note and remind him that when times get tough or the construction market takes a downturn, a product like mine might be even more valuable. I always leave the door open for another try."

Reality Check

WHAT IF THEY JUST DON'T LIKE YOUR IDEA?

Times of change are good times for selling with ideas but some customers are just resistant. Guy Kawasaki, who was marketing director at Apple Computer when the Macintosh was launched, said, "I've come to learn that if people don't get the idea very quickly, just move on. To some people the Macintosh was nothing but a computer, but to some small segment of the world, it was very exciting. If they don't get your idea, just move on. Don't let the bozos grind you down."

When Brigham gets rejected she also moves on but gives her customers something to think about: "I tell them I'm going down their street to tell other folks about what my products can do for them. Since they're in the same business, it's possible that on a competitive bid, another electrical contractor may be using my products. So I tell him, 'If the time comes that you lose a project to someone else based on the cost savings we've discussed, I hope you'll call me.' "

Frank Pinto, vice president worldwide sales of Sun Microsystems, describes a more passive way to deal with change-resistant customers, "In the fast-paced information technology marketplace, we just sit and wait for them to replaced. Usually it takes about eighteen months and they're gone."

Application Question

How can I create my own idea currency by finding fresh and interesting ideas to share with my customers?

8

Motivating Your Customer by
Selling Value

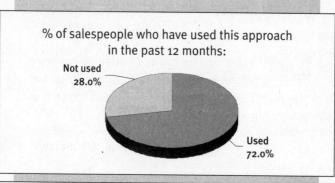

% of salespeople who have used this approach
in the past 12 months:

Not used
28.0%

Used
72.0%

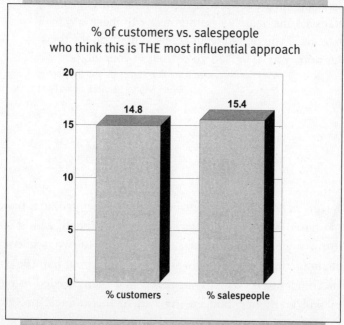

% of customers vs. salespeople
who think this is THE most influential approach

14.8

15.4

% customers

% salespeople

"To sell value today you have to point out why your product is legitimately better than another product. In some situations the differences between products are perceptual. I'm not sure that bottled Evian water is any different from New York City tap water, but there is certainly a perception that it is."

HENRY BERGSOM, president, National Electrical Manufacturers Representatives Association

"Customers want value, just as you and I do when we make our personal acquisitions. We will look at the price but there's after-sale service, reputation, and brand image that all play a very big role."

BILL ETHERINGTON, senior vice president and group executive of sales and distribution group, IBM Corporation

"It is inappropriate to leave a client with the responsibility to translate the value you're portraying to them into their own terms. If you present your case and don't do the translation work, you've missed 70 percent of your job."

MARTY SUNDE, managing director, sales and marketing, Enron Energy Services Operations

A client friend of mine invented the perfect product. It was based on an exciting technical breakthrough, would outperform any product in its market by a factor of two, and could be manufactured and brought to market for about half the cost of its competition. When I suggested that there needed to be a sales and marketing budget attached to this miracle product, my client balked and said, "I've built a much more valuable mousetrap; customers will beat a path to my door."

After two years of good sales and steady growth, a much larger company announced plans to build a similar product. This competitor had a formidable sales force and marketing machine that created such a buzz for their nonexistent product that my client found himself on the defensive, fighting a perception that he was just a "flash in the pan" company. Sales dropped as customers postponed buying to see what the larger company might offer. A year later, two full years before the bigger company even came out with their product, my client was out of business. He had created a product that clearly offered superior value in terms of features, benefits, and price, but had ignored the intangible side of the sale.

Today, product value is not based on features and benefits alone. It is based on a collection of perceptions about your product that accrues every time the product touches a customer. The only real security in product value lies in the collective minds of your customer base. Building a better mousetrap is only the first step. Building a better *perception* of your mousetrap is the second.

OLD THINKING	To sell value convert product features into benefits, then sell the benefits.
WHAT'S DIFFERENT	Unique features don't stay unique for long, so building value on them is dangerous.
NEW THINKING	Value is a perception in the mind of the customer that is created every time your product touches a customer. Selling value is managing that perception.

Approaches

HELP YOUR CLIENT SEE YOUR PRODUCT IN A NEW AND EXCITING WAY

If you can get your customer truly excited about your product, its value to him skyrockets. Not so long ago sales managers believed that if their sales force became wildly enthusiastic about a product, somehow that enthusiasm would transfer to customers. Today, customers have too many nearly equivalent choices and are too sophisticated to get excited just because you are. The thinking on enthusiasm has shifted from how to generate a more enthusiastic salesperson to how to generate excitement within the customer. Some thoughts:

1. Customers get excited about products for their own reasons, not yours

My sales manager's voice crackled with excitement as he unveiled the redesign of our product. "Our new design looks great. It's right at the cutting edge and light-years ahead of our competition. If this doesn't get your customers excited, I don't know what will." I psyched myself up and presented the redesign for the first time. My customer looked at it and looked at it again. Slowly he said, "Well, it's kind of like a new haircut; it takes a little getting used to, but once I do I'm sure it won't be too bad." Later, over a beer, he told me that he appreciated the effort we had put into the redesign but that he viewed this as maintenance he expected of all his best suppliers. The details of keeping a product's look up-to-date were just routine for him and I had wasted a call.

2. Customers get enthusiastic about products for what they can do, not for what they are

There's an old story about a drill-bit salesperson who was very enthusiastic about his product and loved explaining how

his bits were crafted of the finest steel using only the best methods. One day he lost a major sale at a large furniture manufacturer to a rival salesperson who knew far less about steel and
bit making. By chance he encountered this salesperson the next
day and asked him how he had made the sale. His rival replied,
"Your customers will never get excited about drill bits, but do
you know what does get them excited? A half-inch hole in a
piece of wood." The particulars of the product were of very
little interest to this furniture company. They were much more
interested in the results they could achieve from the use of the
product.

If you think this old story isn't true today, think again. One
of Paul Corvino's first sales calls with America Online was a
joint call made with a seasoned AOL salesperson. Recalls Corvino, "We were calling on the president of a department store
whom I had a relationship with from my previous job. Early in
the call my sales rep started explaining why our Web browser
was different from another Web browser. I stopped the conversation and politely asked the president if he knew what a
Web browser was. He admitted that he did not. So there we
were explaining the differences in Web browsers to a person
who didn't know what one was." The president of that department store was really not interested in the technical details
of how America Online works. He wanted to know what kind
of results they could achieve for his business.

3. Build excitement by helping customers see your product in a new way

I once called on a huge distributor—a buyer who was no-
toriously indifferent toward the use of ad space in any way, let
alone seeing ad-space sales reps. I got the appointment with the
understanding that this was a onetime thing, not to be repeated.
I started the call by asking a lot of questions that I prepared
ahead of time. In responding to them, she revealed that her

company did not pay for their own advertising programs. Instead funds were "donated" by the manufacturers whom she represented. This information gave me an idea. I showed her how to design a "product wrap" ad for tabloid publications. These ads consist of a standard-size ad in the lower center of the page; the remaining space is devoted to five small product ads that "wrap" around it. I then suggested that if she ran an ad in the center and "wrapped" it with five small product ads—one for each of her manufacturers—she could make them very happy. She loved the idea and ended up buying a big program. I didn't try to sell her ad space, but instead I got her excited by helping her see my product as a way to make her manufacturing partners happy.

Another time I was trying to sell advertising readership studies to a magazine publisher who was just not buying. He told me that ad readership studies had not been beneficial to him in the past. Later in the conversation he shared his frustration in dealing with his editors. Having no editorial background himself, he always felt his editors were bamboozling him. I pointed out that while my ad readership studies primarily evaluated a publication's ads they also evaluated every major piece of editorial in a magazine. I suggested that he could use this part of the study to evaluate the performance of his editors. He became very excited and bought a yearlong program. I didn't try to sell him an ad readership study. Instead I got him excited by helping him see my product as a way to monitor the effectiveness of his editors.

TRANSLATE VALUE INTO THE CUSTOMER'S ENVIRONMENT

To Marty Sunde, managing director of sales and marketing at Enron Services Operation, selling value is about translating offered benefits into the customer's environment. This might sound like the stuff of many casual sales calls, but what Sunde describes is anything but casual. He says, "After we meet with a customer we discuss among ourselves how we can show the dollar impact of this benefit in the customer's environment." Sunde shared an example of this kind of translation work as he justified to a potential customer the benefits of doing business with his company, a company much larger than the one he was competing with: "We went into our meeting and found that the client company has forty-two locations. Through some paperwork we found that those locations were all in places where we have service available twenty-four hours a day, seven days a week. Our research also showed that the client had three shifts operating and that there's a piece of equipment that needs attention on a random basis across all shifts. When this equipment goes down, typically these people would wait until the next day to get the problem fixed. We figured that it costs X amount of money to have this process done for X amount of time, and if that downtime occurs three times a month across forty-two locations, it could amount to a loss of X dollars."

If the difference between working with a big company versus a smaller one had been left at the abstract level, it's likely that Sunde's company might not have gotten the bid. I have seen salespeople successfully argue the merits of big and small companies. A big company has more locations, but sometimes it's better to be a big fish in a small pond. By "translating value," what Sunde's team did was to take the customer's specific situation and show that doing business with a larger company like his was the greater value.

EDUCATE CUSTOMERS ABOUT QUALITY

Twenty-five years ago a huge part of a buyer's job was to determine the qualitative differences between products and suppliers. But in the aftermath of the Japanese quality invasion of America's car industry, the quality and customer-service movements of the past twenty years, and the standardized quality methods like ISO 9000, the difference in quality between products is smaller than ever. As a result, many buyers are not well trained to understand quality differences. Even if they do, their organizations may not care. The attitude in many places is, buy the cheapest you can, as long as the quality is "good enough."

When Cam Bishop, president of Primedia's Intertec Publishing Group, heard about a hole-in-the-wall tailor shop that was selling very high-quality suits at reasonable prices, he dropped by on a whim. Upon arriving, he noticed that the small shop was just down the street from a huge Men's Wearhouse clothing store and that all the proprietor had to sell with were a few samples, a brochure, and some fabric swatches. But the store owner proved to be a quality evangelist who so strongly believed in his products that he took it upon himself to educate anyone who walked into his shop on the quality differences between suits. Said Bishop, "You can't leave his shop without knowing more about quality than you ever knew before. I knew some basics, but now I know about different fabrics, stitches, and some of the little extra things he builds into his suits to make them better." The shop owner came up to Bishop and said, "See this little extra fold of cloth? When your suit is dry-cleaned, the suit's lining can shrink. On this suit, we put a little extra fold of cloth so the suit doesn't pucker if the lining shrinks." Once Bishop understood the quality this small shop provided, he could buy with confidence—he ended up buying two suits when he had walked in with no intention of making a purchase at all.

You can still sell value by showing the quality of your product, but before you do, you have to educate the buyer on what the differences are and why they are important.

BE PREPARED TO SELL YOUR "TOTAL PRODUCT"

In marketing circles today there's talk of the "total product," which includes any aspect of a product that touches your customer in any way. Aside from the actual product or service you deliver, there are many intangibles such as reputation, brand, service, partnerships, industry "buzz," financial news, word on the street about your company, competitive presence, ad campaigns, celebrity status of your CEO, recent turnover in personnel, and news of major sales.

In the information-rich environment your customers operate in, there's just a lot more data about your company and your company's product in circulation—that reaches him in a variety of ways. If word reaches him that your company is about to be sold, it's possible that his perception of your product's value may suffer. News that your company has just hired away three top salespeople from a direct competitor could have the opposite effect.

I have a client who buys only from the hottest companies in the market. He closely monitors personnel changes, stock prices, advertising campaigns, and business news concerning his suppliers and never fails to mention all this whenever I call on him. Sometimes I think he worries more about my business than his own, but this is how he makes value judgments and decides which suppliers to work with. When calling on this client, I try to outscoop him with newspaper clippings, an ad from a breaking advertising campaign, or industry gossip.

Step-by-Step

1. GET OUT OF YOUR MIND AND INTO THEIRS

If value is a perception in the mind of your customer, the first step to selling value is to understand what goes on in her mind. Having worked on many research studies about customer buying, I can tell you that the mind of the customer can be unpredictable. On the surface, it seems stable and predictable enough, but I often find that the sound, rational words customers offer as the reason they made a purchase disguise the underlying motivators. Some good questions to start a dialogue going:

How do you evaluate products in my category?

What parameters are most important?

How do you evaluate quality?

But logical answers to rational questions only begin the process. According to Robert Passikoff, president of Brand Keys, Inc., "Often customers do not really know, other times they don't want to tell you but since you asked they give you an answer that sounds plausible or that they think you want to hear. Finally there are some clients who will give you any old explanation as to how they evaluate products because they just want to get you off their back."

When you ask how a customer evaluates products, sometimes the first thing you hear is not the real answer. Passikoff says, "You need to be able to capture value in ways that reach the emotional as well as the rational underpinnings. It's not as easy as it sounds."

2. LOOK BEYOND IMMEDIATE NEEDS

A flowerpot salesperson, while first calling on a chain of plant stores, asked a buyer if there was anything his current supplier was not providing him. The buyer replied that he needed some bigger pots—large enough to hold a small tree.

The salesperson had discovered a need and ran to the back of his van to get a large pot in an attempt to close a sale. The customer placed a small order, but when the salesperson called back for a reorder order he was turned down. The client replied, "My current supplier actually does have a line of larger pots and they matched your price, so I am staying with them." This scenario might have played out differently had the salesperson kept probing for an understanding of the values behind his customer's immediate need. Why, for example, was there a need for larger pots where there had been no demand before? It turned out that several new housing developments and office buildings had recently been built in the area and large plants were being used for interior decoration. Had the salesperson probed further, he could have discovered that there was an opportunity for this flower shop, not just to buy a few larger pots, but to revisit the entire pot category with regard to their use in interior design. What if the salesperson had gone back to his home office and worked up a program for helping plant shops deal with this new trend? If the salesperson had built a program around a trend, he might have built a business, not just made a quick, onetime sale.

I have seen salespeople miss large sales as they jump on a sale as soon as a need became apparent. Keep asking questions. When a need emerges, that's the time to gain a deeper understanding. If you jump into a product sell, typically the discussion that could lead to a bigger sale stops short.

3. VALUE-MAP YOUR CLIENT'S MIND

When I start selling a new product I sit down and make a list of the important issues that can play a part in a customer's decision on where to buy. This list includes important product features as well as any other parameters. Here's a list I've used to evaluate clients for buying magazine ad space.

HOW DO YOU EVALUATE PUBLICATIONS?

1 = not important   5 = extremely important

Market leadership 1 2 3 4 5

Availability of special positions in magazine 1 2 3 4 5

Well-read editorial 1 2 3 4 5

Editors who favorably write up products 1 2 3 4 5

Circulation size 1 2 3 4 5

Cost 1 2 3 4 5

Ability to generate sales leads 1 2 3 4 5

Graphics/overall look of the product 1 2 3 4 5

Personal relationships 1 2 3 4 5

Readership demographics 1 2 3 4 5

"I like to read it" 1 2 3 4 5

"My boss likes it" 1 2 3 4 5

Publication's brand 1 2 3 4 5

Value added 1 2 3 4 5

Reputation for good service 1 2 3 4 5

Of course, the items on your product's value-map list will be different. After visiting a customer, fill out a form and score him on the different parameters. Once in a while feedback from my customers tells me I need to add a new parameter. This exercise helps focus on understanding where a customer finds value and is a reminder that there are many ways to assign value.

4. VALUE-RATE YOUR OWN INVENTORY

After you've filled out a value map for your customers, take a copy and fill one out for your own products and honestly rate them along all parameters. Now fill out a form to value-rate each of your competitor's products. Sometimes it is hard to be objective. But I have always felt that a salesperson who realistically understands his product's strengths and weaknesses is in a better position to sell it.

5. LISTEN FOR ECCENTRIC EVALUATORS

A client who bought trade-magazine ad space from me surprised me with the question "Do you know what you guys do that I think is really valuable?" I shrugged my shoulders. He spun around in his chair and picked up a stack of sales lead reports that my magazine had generated for him whenever a reader circled a "bingo card" number associated with his ad. Then he dug down through a report and pointed to one tiny number. "There," he said proudly. "That number tells me how many other 'bingo card' numbers a reader has circled at the same time he circled the number for my ad. I use this number to tell me if this guy is really interested in my product, or if he's just a tire kicker who circles every number on the card. Do you realize you're the only publishing company in our industry that provides this number?" I had to confess to him that I didn't. What's worse, this number that constituted the most important point of value for him was buried in pages and pages of data.

Once you get past the rational explanations of how people form value judgments, the terrain can get very scary. Often customers develop unique ways of looking at products that they rarely have an opportunity to articulate to others. During some of my travels I have heard the following:

- "When I buy from salespeople with well-shined shoes I never go wrong."

- "I buy from them because their sales manager looks like my brother-in-law."

- "I buy from them because their ads have a sense of humor."

- "I buy from a national base of suppliers but I always try to buy from suppliers in the Midwest because they're more polite."

Buyers often don't always think rationally about how they are assigning value to products, they just do it. When you probe down deep you'll uncover perceptions that would sound absurd if they were voiced in a professional setting.

6. MAKE SURE IT IS REAL

You have listened to your customer and believe you can present your product in a way that calls attention to its value. When you address value as your customer defines it, you most often have his attention. If instead you start with a preconceived notion of what value "should be," often you get polite nods. I always come right out and ask, "Is this important to you?" If I get a blank stare I ask, "If not this, then what is?"

7. WATCH FOR VALUE SHIFTS

The way your customers evaluate products changes over time. In 1970, Americans buying automobiles picked styling as the most important characteristic to consider. By 1975, with oil prices climbing, fuel economy was most important. In 1980, the emphasis had shifted to quality of construction. In the space of ten years the same group of consumers rating the same product picked different characteristics as most important in evaluating the product for purchase. This is true of any product. How customers assign value to products can change quickly. According to Robert Passikoff, president of Brand Keys, "More often than not, when values in a category change, people move quickly and don't think or talk about it very much. By the time they are able and willing to talk about it, very often it's too late." Passikoff is concerned that even salespeople in the front line are not always going to get the message. He says, "Even though the sales folks are on the front line, the longer they deal with a category, the greater the likelihood they don't really know what the customer wants." It's important to ask questions of your customers again and again and to maintain a current understanding of how they are evaluating products in your area. If you think you have a perfect understanding of a customer, get ready for change.

8. ASSUMPTIONS ARE DANGEROUS

Assuming that you know how a customer assigns value is dangerous. Too often I have walked into a customer's office with a preconceived idea of this only to be surprised. I have heard salespeople say of their territories, "All my customers want is a lower price," or, "If we could just get them this one feature they would all buy what I'm selling." I believe that value is a far more complex issue than that. Selling the intrinsic value of your product means understanding what your customer wants beyond her immediate needs. It means understanding her value system and what kinds of things are important to her when she looks at products in your category. It also means understanding customers as people, understanding how they work on an emotional level, understanding what practical matters are a priority to them, and understanding how all of this can turn on a dime when circumstances change. You also need to understand your product and the different ways it can be presented within the context of the customer's point of view. In today's fast-moving, image-driven marketplace, value is a perception that exists in the mind of your customer.

Reality Check

WHAT IF MY CUSTOMER DOES NOT WANT TO BUY QUALITY?

In today's marketing environment the word "quality" has been so overused that it has little meaning. All customers want quality but it means something different to everyone. When a customer tells you he does not care about the quality of what you are selling him, stop and listen. Most of the time he's giving you clues as to what is valuable. Your job is to build a selling dialogue around that. But there are times when customers just want the cheapest product they can to get by. If you are not in a position to provide this, then move on to the next customer.

WHAT IF ALL MY CUSTOMER WANTS TO TALK ABOUT IS PRICE, PRICE, PRICE!

Often when a customer tells you your price is too high she is really telling you that her perception of the value of your product is too low. I have used two approaches to sell value to the price grinder.

1. Lead her through a value talk to get to the price
Say, "Okay, I talked to my manager and have a price I can offer you, but just so you understand what we have done for you I need to explain our pricing." Typically this gets a cus-

tomer's attention. Then you lead her through a discussion about the value points of your product, each time mentioning that "this costs us money, so it is built into the price. Since we hire only the best people, here are their credentials, etc." Finally, after you have woven your value points into the talk, give her the price and conclude, "In light of all the extra value we present, I hope you will agree that this is a terrific price considering what you are getting."

2. Anticipate the price objection and sell, sell, sell before it comes up

Once the price objection is brought up, the psychology of the call changes. Anything you do to sell value often sounds like a defensive move to justify your price. You simply have to do all of your value selling early. Once price comes up, it's too late.

Application Question

How can I create a perception of value for my product in my customer's mind?

9

Motivating Your Customer by
Networking

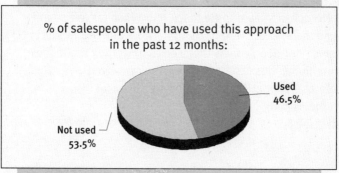

% of salespeople who have used this approach
in the past 12 months:

Used
46.5%

Not used
53.5%

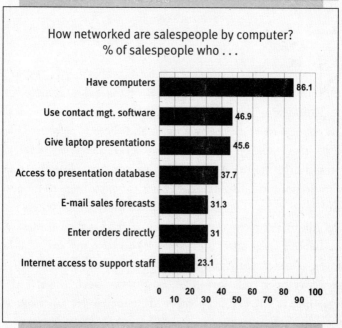

How networked are salespeople by computer?
% of salespeople who . . .

Have computers	86.1
Use contact mgt. software	46.9
Give laptop presentations	45.6
Access to presentation database	37.7
E-mail sales forecasts	31.3
Enter orders directly	31
Internet access to support staff	23.1

0 10 20 30 40 50 60 70 80 90 100

"The hands-down, most efficient way for our agents to meet quality prospects is through referral, word of mouth, one person to the next."

BILL BECKLEY, executive vice president of agencies, Northwestern Mutual Life

"There doesn't seem to be much reluctance for our people to use their personal contacts to network and sell products because our people view themselves as getting the money a traditional business would spend on advertising. And that's really what they are—they're the advertising arm, and the training arm."

KEN McDONALD, senior vice president, managing director–The Americas, Amway Corp.

New personal communications technology has transformed the traditional tools of the business networker. The Rolodex is being replaced by contact management software, handwritten notes by e-mail, and the business-card file by the address book on your Web browser. It has never been easier to build and maintain a network of contacts. But these same technologies have also made it easier for customers to hide from unsolicited calls. The question I hear most often when I give talks about problem clients is, "How do I get customers who hide behind voice mail and caller ID to take my calls?" Maintaining contact with good customers—those with whom you have developed relationships—has never been easier. At the same time it's never been more difficult to get to those who choose to hide.

In the new customer-empowered world you are either on the

inside or on the outside of your customer's network. One way to get by the voice-mail problem is to become part of your customer's network so that he will take the time to use these empowering communication technologies to include you in his dialogue. Salespeople are reinventing the traditional approaches to networking to take advantage of these trends. While building a traditional network of personal contacts is always a terrific idea, the big wins for salespeople lie in working their *customers'* networks.

OLD THINKING	Building your own personal network is a great way to increase sales.
WHAT'S DIFFERENT	New technology has empowered customers to communicate and network with a limited group of salespeople and exclude all others.
NEW THINKING	You are either inside your customer's network or outside it. Selling is no longer about building up your own network, it's about breaking into your customer's network.

Approaches

USE NETWORK MOMENTUM TO SELL

If you stop thinking of your sales territory as a collection of individual customers and start thinking of them as a customer network, selling opportunities begin to present themselves. When Jodi Stern, marketing director for Vin Divino, first started visiting Washington, D.C., to sell her company's line of high-end Austrian wines, she viewed the area as a networked group of customers. Instead of targeting the larger wine stores that

sold the most wine, she mapped out a plan based on her understanding of the interaction between the members of the wine-
buying community in that city. She started with top restaurants
in the area. Wine buyers frequented these spots to try wines,
though the actual number of bottles sold was quite low. Over
time she managed to get her wines into the top six restaurants
in the city. After this first wave of acceptance, the word on her
wines began to filter through the community. As her customers
talked to other customers, she gained access to locations where
larger-volume sales could be made. By viewing her customers
as a networked group, she was able to start her own momentum
and ride it through the buying community to meet her goals.

TARGET A CUSTOMER'S NETWORKED FRIENDS

I once had a very tough account whose rep refused to buy
from me. He was one of the largest buyers in my territory and
so selling him was a priority. Through his secretary I discovered
that he used to work at a much smaller account of mine where
he still maintained close friendships. I made it a priority to
spend time with the buyer of that small account. As our relationship developed there, the buyer with the larger account began to warm to me. Eventually I got to know the buyer at the
small company well enough to have a conversation about his
friend. When I mentioned that I was having difficulty starting
a dialogue, my new friend smiled a big smile and said, "So, is
my friend Jimmy giving you a hard time? Why he's just a big
teddy bear. I'll have a talk with him." My new friend did have
a talk with Jimmy and my relationship with him took a sharp
turn for the better. But it wasn't Jimmy whom I sold first—it
was one of the key members of his network.

TARGET NETWORK CLUSTERS

In every territory I have ever worked, there were clusters of customers who regularly talked to each other. These little networks form spontaneously for a wide variety of reasons. The challenge is to find them and then spend whatever amount of time it takes to make a favorable impression on any one of its members. I know that if I do something incredible for one member of a tight network, word will spread.

Some examples of these tight-knit networks:

1. "We used to work there."

When Central Dynamics went out of business its former employees scattered throughout the greater Toronto area. As I travel throughout this area I call on at least a dozen small manufacturers with key personnel who used to work at that company. Over the years I've gotten to know some of these former employees and built strong relationships with them. When I bump into yet another Central Dynamics alumnus I mention some of my friends who also used to work there. Invariably, after I leave, they call their friends, get a favorable reaction, and I am well along the way toward building credibility and making sales.

2. "You've got a reputation."

A friend of mine worked as an attorney for the state of New York for many years before deciding to hang a shingle and practice on his own. His first year out was a struggle as he scrambled to get clients anywhere he could. One day he handled a divorce case for a Korean-American. He did such a great job that before he knew it, he was handling many divorces for Korean-Americans throughout New York City. He never planned on becoming the premier divorce lawyer in the Korean-

American community there, but his standout work for that early client plugged him into a network eager for his services.

3. "A business cluster within an industry"

In the world of broadcast television equipment, there's a small enclave of people who manufacture and sell transmitters for TV stations. It is a highly specialized field in which the people at competitive companies know each other well. I've never seen anyone from a transmitter company at some point leave and go to work at another kind of television equipment company for long. Such clusters within industries are little networked worlds. If you make a favorable impression on one buyer, word travels fast.

NETWORKING WITHIN A CUSTOMER BASE

Mike McGrail, president of the McGrail Group, thinks that networking is the way smaller companies can compete with larger firms. Says McGrail, "The very large firms tend to have immediate credibility. But very small firms can still market themselves successfully through word of mouth and networking." McGrail has made a significant commitment to this effort. He and his wife together put in about a hundred and thirty hours of networking time per month. And it has paid off. McGrail once met the general manager of a large company at a church function. He maintained the acquaintance over time, until one day the GM asked McGrail what he did for a living. McGrail told him, and was invited to make a presentation. He got the account and it went on to be one of his biggest. One day he asked a vice president at the account how many different training companies had tried to secure the business that McGrail had locked in. The vice president said that there were literally thousands. Networking builds a relationship before you do business. In other words, people get to know you before they even know they need you. When it comes time to hire a supplier, you are a familiar, perhaps trusted face, which can put you ahead of the field.

BUILD YOUR OWN NETWORK SUPPORT STAFF WITHIN YOUR ORGANIZATION

According to Neil Rackham, author of *Rethinking the Sales Force,* the separation between sales and service is vanishing. Salespeople must now excel at mustering internal resources to service customer needs.

I know many elite salespeople who butt heads with their support staffs and later regret it. They think that since they control the customer revenue stream, the "lowly" support people are there to do their bidding. But smart salespeople take the time to build their own internal networks of support staff who are happy to do them a favor if an angry customer pops up and needs their attention quickly. Customers value salespeople who can exert internal influence on their own organizations and respond quickly to service requests.

SELL BY EXTENDING YOUR NETWORK

Al Ries, of Ries and Ries Focusing Consultants, recalls how a printer's salesperson helped by integrating Ries into his own personal network. When Ries was just starting out as a public speaker, this salesperson suggested he join an executive club so he could gain exposure to a whole group of people who might hire him. He even introduced Ries to the club president. He recalls, "Buying printing is buying a commodity, but this salesperson helped me in ways that went beyond his product." The result? "We bought a lot of printing from him."

SPONSOR A NETWORKING EVENT

Through a chance meeting at a European trade show, I had the opportunity to chat with the newly appointed president of Sony Broadcast & Professional Company, Ed Grebow. Perhaps because I knew Grebow from his previous job he casually extended a dinner invitation to join him and a few friends. He scribbled the address on the back of his business card. That evening when I pulled out Grebow's card I found that the event was being held in a private room on the top floor of the exclusive Akura Hotel in Amsterdam. When I arrived I found that Grebow's "few friends" included the top technical managers from CNN, CBS, NBC, Informix, and Turner Entertainment, as well as the top people from Sony and three industry publications. The Akura Hotel staff served a spectacular seven-course dinner as we looked out over the Amsterdam skyline.

The conversation was anything but casual. Grebow took center stage and posed thought-provoking questions to the entire group. After a memorable evening the new president had helped solidify his network and expand those of his guests. Grebow later told me, "I do dinners like that at industry events to encourage industry leaders to meet and discuss important issues. In today's business climate, relationships are everything, and I try to help my friends meet the people they should know."

Step-by-Step

No matter where you are directing your networking activities, the skill set is pretty much the same. Here are the basics:

1. IDENTIFY THE NETWORK YOU WANT TO PENETRATE

The first step to selling a network is to trace its outlines. Whenever I take over a new sales territory I ask, "Who knows whom?" If you start viewing your territory as a networked collection of customers, as opposed to a collection of individuals who happen to be buying from the same source, you'll have a better understanding of what's going on. As you first meet with your new customers, determine the answers to some of the following questions to help you identify where these connections might be:

A. Where did they work before they came here?

Often when individuals job-hop they come from organizations in related industries. Chances are good that if they worked at another company for a number of years, they maintain relationships, either formally or informally, with people who still work there.

B. Whom do they consider their competitors?

Some of my clients watch their competitors far more closely than their customers and make a lot of decisions—including buying decisions—based on the behavior of their competitors. If you are looking to map external influences on your customer base, finding out who their competitors are is an excellent first step.

C. Are they involved in any industry associations?

If you can understand where your customer has networks within your industry or category, you will understand the kind of connections he already has.

D. Whom do they respect in the industry or category?

Very often they will mention people with whom you may already have associations or friendships.

2. TARGET YOUR NETWORKING ACTIVITY CAREFULLY

If you are going to commit a significant amount of time to networking, it's important that you target a community that has the potential to return business to you. If you are in a non-industry-specific profession, such as selling accounting services, you might target groups within a certain income bracket. If you are networking in an industry and you have targeted specific accounts, joining an industry association where these accounts gather together is a logical move.

3. ACT THE PART

Among Hollywood producers there is no less desirable company than that of newly arrived actors. These aspiring Hollywood stars arrive by the busload from all over the world, desperate for any contact with producers and directors who might give them their big break. During my three years in Hollywood the producers and directors I worked with would run for cover as soon as these folks appeared on the horizon. At a party my production company threw I was shocked to encounter an unknown, aspiring actor mingling with the very group who would normally have avoided him like the plague. Somehow he had made his way onto their restricted guest list. He came off like a regular guy, not a desperate actor. In addition, he knew all the buzzwords people on the producer/director side of the industry liked to throw around. He knew all about script development and budgeting and did not talk about actors' training. In short, he was not acting like an actor, he was acting like a production person, and he fit in beautifully.

If you, as a salesperson, want to penetrate the networks in which your customers travel, commit yourself to fitting in. That means learning their language, understanding their problems, and finding some way to fit in. Don't talk and act like a salesperson; learn to talk and act like one of their peers.

4. DON'T EXPECT AN IMMEDIATE RETURN

One of the most remarkable networkers I've ever seen is Skip Boucher, president of Vibrint Technologies. A few years ago Vibrint was a start-up company with few employees and prospects. Skip came from a much larger company, where he had developed many business relationships over the years. Consequently he was able to get in to see most of them when the time came to sell the concept of his new company. Boucher recalls that it was easy in the beginning because these were people with whom he had already invested a lot of time. "I didn't have to do a lot of convincing because we had a previous relationship. I did call on several companies where I had no relationships and those were much tougher. Although I did visit with them and try to convince them to buy in, they didn't buy immediately. It took seeing the other companies going with us to make them come around." Although Boucher's network enabled him to get his start-up company going quickly, he insists it wasn't a long-term plan. He never thought he would someday need these relationships to start up a company. Said Boucher, "I have friends whom I don't hear from unless they need something. That approach doesn't work well in networking. I always make it a point to see people just to say hello whether there is a need to or not. It's hard to do networking when you're under pressure to make the next sale."

5. BE PREPARED TO THINK LONG TERM

According to Mike McGrail, "Networking really is a long-term issue. Networking does not work in the instant-gratification sales environment. It's not the question of going to an organization you join, showing up and saying, 'Who can I sell today?' In our environment of networking, we're after long-term relationships with companies and we're willing to invest the time to build trust and credibility, which might take many years. At various times I've looked at the people we currently work with and think about how long the selling cycle took. It has ranged from six months to three years."

6. ASK YOURSELF WHAT YOU CAN DO FOR OTHER PEOPLE

As a seller, it's easy to think about what a buyer can do for you, but it's harder when you turn the statement around. There is no question that people will buy from you first if you have given them something of value first. Viewed this way, networking is a form of informal reciprocity. So the question is, as you begin your networking, what can *you* do for these people? Sometimes it's helpful to make a list. If you are approaching a group with common interests, maybe there is an article or a piece of information that you can mail to people or share in person. If you call on a group of people with similar business interests, keep an eye on the job market so that when one of your customers is looking for a new position, you have a ready suggestion. Look out for opportunities that come up within your own organization to buy things in beneficial ways. You can give the prospective customers advice on how to deal with business situations or even family situations. In my career as a salesperson I have helped numerous colleagues find jobs, rework résumés, land new customers by intervening directly on their behalf, find new office space, find a literary agent, generate ideas for an advertising campaign, find new support staff, and the list goes on. Very often what you're doing is putting people who have a need in touch with people who have a solution. Often it has nothing to do with the product you are selling. The more people you help, the more help you'll get when you need it.

7. POSITION YOURSELF

All of us have been in meetings where someone at the table says, "What we really need is someone who can repair used widgets" (or something like that). Now, from your networking you may know somebody who repairs old widgets. But if that person hadn't told you about his work, his name would not come up and he would miss the business opportunity. The challenge is to present yourself in a simple memorable way so that when people encounter a broken widget, they think of you. A very easy way to do this is to explain what it is you do when you introduce yourself. "Hi, I'm John and I can fix any widget that ever existed."

8. IDENTIFY OTHER NETWORKERS

Within every industry in which I have sold, there are people who spend a lot of time networking and are consequently extremely well connected. As soon as I identify these people, I spend whatever time it takes to get them sold on what I'm doing. Often if you can win these people over you'll feel their influence well beyond the sales you make to their specific company. If one customer's name keeps coming up over and over again as you try to identify network connections within your targeted sales territory, that person is someone to pay special attention to. The long-term rewards can be tremendous.

9. SYSTEMATICALLY FEED YOUR NETWORK

I keep all my client contacts on a contact management software package. Every so often I send them all a joke I come across on the Internet. When I do, I get dozens of responses within hours. People I haven't heard from in a while are reminded of me and the services I provide. An important thing is not to have these communications viewed as a solicitation for business, but rather as something sent out for entertainment and enjoyment.

10. NETWORKING THROUGH REFERRALS

According to Fran Jacoby, president of The Jacoby Agency, getting referrals is a straightforward process. "Doing it is really quite simple. All you have to do is ask. But I never ask anyone for a referral until I've completed their work and they really trust and like me. Sometimes I'll even feed them the name of a person I'd like to meet. I usually give them the name of someone that I know that they know and say I have really been waiting a long time to meet so-and-so and I know that you know them fairly well. If you wouldn't mind setting up a breakfast for the three of us . . . most people say that's fine, I don't mind."

11. START TO CREATE YOUR OWN COMMUNITY

The best way to work a network of customers is to create it yourself. When job positions become open, if you can help fill them with referrals from your own network, you can begin to shape your territory, not just sell to it. In addition, you can create interactions between your customer base by sponsoring wine parties or functions that encourage customers who are satisfied with your work to communicate with one another. Try taking multiple customers who share common interests out to dinner and introducing them to one another.

Selling your territory as a network is a terrific way to motivate customers to buy from you. As your customers network among themselves they will amplify positive messages about you and your product or services across the network. It's a terrific indirect way to reinforce the benefits that you have to offer. It also reduces call resistance and creates an aura of acceptance throughout an industry. Suddenly cold calls made to initiate new business are no longer met with indifference. You might say, "Well, we already do business with your sister company, why don't you ask George about us?" If your name and your product's name seem to pop up ubiquitously throughout an industry, even insecure buyers nervous about keeping their jobs will buy your product fearlessly.

Reality Check

I HAVE SPENT ALL THIS TIME GETTING TO KNOW PEOPLE AND NO ONE HAS REFERRED ANY BUSINESS MY WAY? WHAT'S WRONG?

What's most often wrong is that you haven't demonstrated proof of your worth. You met someone at a networking event and swapped cards, but how does the other person know you are competent? It is one thing to hand out a phone number but quite another to take the risk of recommending someone. Yet insider recommendations are what make the difference. Swapping records is where networking begins, but until the person who receives your card is convinced you offer real value, the connection will not go further. What needs to accompany the card swap is some kind of proof that you can deliver on your promise or have an experience that demonstrates some kind of expertise. In network clubs, the real networking often occurs on committees as people get a chance to actually work with each other.

Application Question

How can I become a part of my customer's network?

10

Motivating Your Customer by
Building Relationships

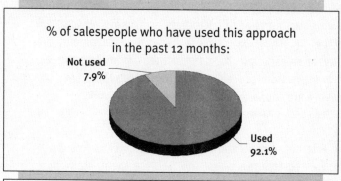

% of salespeople who have used this approach in the past 12 months:

Not used
7.9%

Used
92.1%

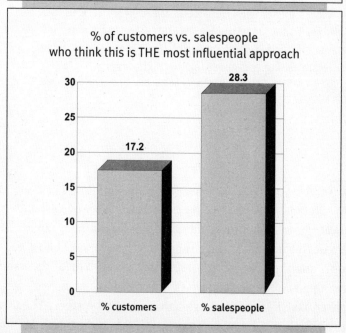

% of customers vs. salespeople
who think this is THE most influential approach

17.2

28.3

% customers

% salespeople

"If you take care of your customer first, everything else, even in a big corporation, takes care of itself."

LEE IACOCCA, chairman and founder, EV Global Motors

"There are some customers whose buying is more and more transactional; they will squeeze on price, don't want to talk to salespeople, and would rather do business electronically. But an equal number of customers want more advice than ever before. They expect more in-depth involvement, the ability of salespeople to marshal their internal resources, and want customized solutions. The salespeople who are surviving are those who can do this kind of work."

NEIL RACKHAM, president of Huthwaite, Inc., and creator of SPIN Selling

"The Internet, e-mail, and Web pages are means to supplement face-to-face meetings — not replace them. Many people have mistakenly replaced these for face-to-face meetings. Today, face-to-face meetings are even more important, interesting, and powerful. The irony is that most people are falling too much for the digital realm."

GUY KAWASAKI, CEO of Garage.com and author of *Selling the Dream*

Twelve years ago, at a meeting of media buyers just outside Philadelphia, the speaker asked for a show of hands to indicate how audience members evaluated the magazines they were buying ad space from. When the speaker asked how many people analyzed magazine circulation, about half of the hands went up; about one quarter of the hands went up when the speaker asked how many evaluated editorial quality. Then the speaker smiled a knowing smile and said, "Okay, I've got one more for you. How many of you just buy ad space from the sales reps you like the best?" Every hand in the room went up.

Not that long ago the relationship side of selling was simple. Customers bought from their friends. Their management often encouraged this, thinking that the best way to have a supplier take care of them was to have a friend on the inside.

But today some companies actively discourage buyers from befriending salespeople. According to Tony Pecoraro, vice president sales at Nordic Ware, "Twenty years ago you could take a buyer to dinner, send him something for the holidays, and become very, very close. But today, there are companies where I can't even buy a client a soda because it is against company policy. At other companies, gratuities of any kind are limited or forbidden."

Bruce Himelstein, senior vice president of sales for North America, Marriott, said of this change, "Suddenly there was a new generation of clients who were CPAs, attorneys, or members of a buying committee. You had to do more than play a round of golf or slap them on the back; you had to bring value to their business." Although friendship alone will no longer carry the sale, the relationship a salesperson develops with a client is more important than ever before because it is more demanding. Once the buyer/seller relationship was largely a one-way communication that funneled sales messages to a customer. But today, that same relationship may now be used to develop complex, value-added programs, partnership programs, or carry important feedback back to the home office. Today, the relationship is more interactive. At times more information flows from the customer to the home office than the other way around.

OLD THINKING Buyers buy from their friends. As the saying goes, "Two people who like each other will always find a way to do business."

WHAT'S DIFFERENT Companies demand value and accountability of their buyers. Some actively discourage developing relationships with salespeople.

- -

NEW THINKING Relationship building is a two-step process. In the first step the salesperson builds a logical case for business and earns the customer's respect. After that he has earned the right to develop a friendship.

Approaches

SELL FROM THE INSIDE OUT

While selling advertising space for a technical engineering magazine, I was invited to the planning meeting for the launch of a customer's new product. I was not there to sell anything; I was there to advise them on making their launch a success.

This company let me, a salesperson, into a sensitive discussion long before anyone was even thinking about buying ad space because I had spent years building a relationship with this company. The people in the room trusted me, respected and valued my opinion, and felt that whatever bias I would bring into the room would always be tempered with the understanding that their needs came first.

Along with the broad-stroke plans the group discussed were two seemingly minor issues. First, the vice president of marketing asked the group if they should put the biggest emphasis on trade advertising or direct mail. It was no surprise to anyone that I spoke in favor of using trade advertising. But the points I made were valid, helpful for the client, and after a spirited discussion, carried the day. The second issue came up when the ad manager asked how the marketing messages should be structured for the target audience. Should the messages be put in technical terms or should they adopt a more image-oriented approach? I advocated a more technical approach since the product being sold was largely bought by engineers. While I would benefit directly if they pursued my recommendations, I presented my views solely because they were in the best interest of the client.

Because I had an insider's relationship, I was invited to a meeting where the very parameters of buying in my product area were being discussed. While in that meeting I was able to bring up points that might have been overlooked, points that created preference for my product. It might sound like I was in the driver's seat, but in truth, I thought carefully before arguing my positions. If I acted in a clearly self-serving way, my credibility would be shot and so would my chances of being influential at that level ever again.

The ultimate goal for a salesperson is to develop the kind of relationship where your clients so value your perspective that you're invited to just such a meeting. If you sell air-conditioner maintenance contracts to hospitals, consider that sometime there will be a meeting to discuss whether to hire full-time employees to handle repairs and maintenance or to go outside and hire a contractor. If you sell athletic shoes to department stores, consider that sometime there will be a meeting to discuss how much floor space each of their stores should give to athletic shoes versus other footwear. If you can be involved in these meetings, you can exercise far more influence.

I had the same kind of relationship on a much smaller account. In this case the meeting was with an individual rather than a group and the discussion much less complex. I met with her once a year and she would tell me what her overall budget was and what she had budgeted for my product area. She said to me, "Josh, you know the products in your area better than anyone and I trust your judgment and that you will look out for my best interest. How should I spend my money?" In essence, because I had developed an insider's relationship with this client over the years, she came to rely on me to help her set her budget. She realized that I was a valuable resource who could be trusted to create a plan that would be in her and her company's best interest.

To exercise this level of influence requires a huge amount of effort at long-term relationship building. You have to learn enough about your customer's business to become a valued peer, earn his trust so that he will share confidential information and see that the personal chemistry works between you. If this comes together, your client will consciously accept your influence because he understands you both have something to gain.

In my best territories, in my best years, I felt successful if I could have that kind of relationship with 20 percent of my accounts. In the future that may not be enough. At IBM, Bill Etherington, senior vice president and group executive of the sales and distribution group, shoots for this level of influence every time by investing in high-level people from targeted industries to represent them. Says Etherington, "We bring in very highly skilled people who can talk to the customer in their own terms. The gentleman who manages our relationships with banks in Asia was president of his own bank. We have media people who call on media companies and petroleum people who call on petroleum companies. They understand their client's language and their problems and can identify the issues that the client is dealing with and translate them back to IBM."

DEVELOP BUSINESS EMPATHY

Years ago I traveled to Chicago to an industry function where I met our company's Chicago representative. When the discussion drifted to our sales approaches, he took a dispassionate view and said, "I don't have to know anything about my customer's business or their products, I just have to know how to sell."

I noticed how our behavior differed at this function. Even though Chicago was his home territory and not mine, I had lots to discuss with our customers who were there and spent most of my time mingling with them. My Chicago counterpart sat on the sidelines chatting with other people on our staff. Six months later, after failing to make any progress in his territory, he was let go.

Selling today means making a commitment to develop business empathy for your customers. It means putting yourself in your customer's shoes and seeing, understanding, and feeling the world from his point of view. A major client once told me, "Internally, once we set a buying goal, it is rare that a salesperson comes in and influences this decision in a significant way. But the few salespeople who can do this explain things to us with a deep understanding of our internal requirements."

Having business empathy means you have an intuitive understanding of what your customers are challenged by and what they are looking for. If your company is introducing a new product, the selling will go much more smoothly if your sales staff is so plugged into the minds and hearts of their customers that they know immediately if they have the right tools to make the sale.

Companies are starting to view business empathy as a high priority when they train their salespeople. According to Howard Stevens, CEO of the HR Chally Group, the nature of sales training is going through a huge reevaluation. Says Stevens, "Today sales organizations spend 90 percent of their training dollars on sales skill training—like overcoming objections—and only about 10 percent on understanding their customer's business. But within five years that number will grow to 20 percent, and by the year 2010 about 60 percent of sales training dollars will be spent on teaching salespeople how to understand their customer's business."

This approach is not without its challenges. Says David Fortanbary, director of cardiovascular marketing at Bristol-Myers Squibb, "To sell effectively today, you almost have to become the customer, looking at their business from their perspective, seeing the pressure points, and feeling their issues. The biggest challenge my sales team would have is that sometimes we would get so close to the customers that we forget about our own needs. I would constantly pull my people back and say, 'No, this has to be a win-win-win—for Bristol-Myers Squibb, the physician, and the patient.' "

If you can have an empathetic understanding of how your customer will react to a proposal before you get to a meeting, you have a tremendous advantage.

PRACTICE "THE ART OF CONNECTING"

Sometimes the key to making a sale is not about your issues or your clients', but rather about whether a connection can be made between the two. Jim Schroer, vice president of global marketing at Ford, thinks that the emphasis on selling should not be on technique but on the art of connecting to customers. Says Schroer, "We don't think there's a list of steps you can take to sell anymore. Today, the customer is in control of the sales process, so you have to connect with his needs or her needs better than your competition. If you do this connection job better, you will sell your product, but the process is not about selling, it's about connecting." Schroer says that the art of connecting is half-emotional and half-analytical. On the emotional side, if you can understand your customer's intangible needs and desires, you can relate to him in a way that will make him prefer dealing with you. The analytical side is based on research so you can understand what the customer is looking for in tangible terms—what features he wants and how much he is willing to pay. But the real gain is in joining the emotional and analytical together. Says Schroer, "I'd say the people who are best at selling today are a good balance of both the empathetic and the analytic. They understand customers on a deep emotional basis, but can marry all the facts and figures and offer up a smart, intelligent solution."

USING RELATIONSHIPS AS VALUE SHORTCUTS

Says Marjorie Fagan, vice president, operations/media at Maier Advertising, "It is so hard to be a buyer these days because there is so much information. I get tons of mail, voice mail, and e-mail and feel like I am being bombarded. The salesperson who can step in and quickly point out where the value is for me is a great help. Often buyers lose interest while going through the enormous amount of information before they find the important parts. I need someone to help me cut to the chase." Being able to do this comes from having a deep understanding of customer needs.

Step-by-Step

1. WHY INVEST?

In the beginning, every seller wants a great relationship with every buyer. But whether or not a relationship can develop is strictly in the buyer's control. Every buyer wonders if an investment of time is going to be useful and might ask himself, "Will I get more out of the buying process if I invest the time to develop a relationship with him or should I just buy what I want and move on?" For one-shot sales, investing the time in a relationship may be a waste. As a salesperson, the first sale you have to make is to sell yourself.

There are times when the salesperson also has to ask the time investment question. Sellers today have far more value added to share with customers than ever. Understanding this, the best buyers make selling themselves as valuable customers a priority. In my territories, the buyers who get the best from me are ones who constantly sell the idea that having them as a customer is a benefit to my organization. I have seen this dynamic confuse some seasoned salespeople. In the old days an extremely friendly relationship with a customer often meant that big sales were on the way. I recall a terribly ineffective sales rep who told me she had an "incredible" relationship with a client. The client always seemed on the verge of giving her a huge order. As a result, she saw to it that this client got a lot of value-added services in anticipation of a large order that never materialized.

2. UNDERSTANDING BEGINS WITH PREPARATION

The fastest way to convince a buyer that you are worth the investment of time is to show up well prepared. Buyers don't have the time they once had to educate new salespeople. Says Bruce Himelstein, senior vice president of sales for North America, Marriott, "We don't call up people and say, 'Tell me about your business.' If you haven't taken the time to do your homework, your customer might say, 'Why don't you learn about this on your own time, not mine?' " Himelstein asks, "Have you gone to their Web page? Have you read their annual report? Do you know what the company is about? Have they been in the news lately? Do you know what their stock is at? Do you know the latest bylaws at the association they are dealing with or what their challenges are? If you know all that then pick up the phone." The days when you could show up and ask a customer a lot of introductory questions about their business are over.

3. HOW DOES YOUR CUSTOMER WANT TO BE SOLD?

Cookie-cutter selling with canned pitches is no longer effective. Today, every call is a unique event. Here are several scales I use to help get my bearings.

A. Some clients like to be sold and others like to buy

I have a client who loves to be pursued for every sale he gives me. We have been doing business for years and his buying patterns have become so predictable that we joke about the exact days of the year when he will buy from me. But when I do call for an order it suddenly becomes a very serious occasion during which he pretends that I may not get the order. This client, a master salesperson himself, loves the feeling of being sold.

I have other clients who hate to be sold. They like to consider the facts I present them and take pride in making their own decisions. When I meet a new customer, in the back of my head I'm always thinking, "Does this person want to be sold or does she want to buy?"

B. Some clients are best sold through a logical approach; some need an emotional approach

Some clients will buy from you when it "feels right." These people buy on intuition or through their "gut." For them, the emotional side of the buy is most important. On some level they have to feel the buy is right or it will never go through.

I have also had customers who buy strictly on the facts, preferring a much more logical approach. They like to see numbers, proof before they buy.

C. Some clients buy through people and some buy through specs

I had a client who once explained to me that he considered himself a good judge of character. He felt that he would never be able to visit my company's home office, meet all the people there, or understand all of the product specs being presented to him. But he could evaluate the caliber of the salesperson whom the company sent to call on him. If he was impressed by their representative, he would be impressed by the organization. This client bought through relationships. I have another client who bases his purchase decisions on the product specs. He carefully analyzes all the numbers and reports. Then he goes into a room, closes the door, weighs the facts against one another, and makes a choice. Says Bob Raleigh, president Domestic Television Distribution, Carsey-Werner, "I have a mantra that says if you listen well enough, your customer will tell you what they need to be sold. That can be solving their problems, marketing a brand, building a comfort or safety factor because they are insecure, or a wide variety of other things. The goal is presenting your product in a way that is consistent with what motivates that person."

4. PUT RELATIONSHIPS BEFORE TRANSACTIONS

A sales rep calling on a company president I know told him in the first five minutes of a sales call, "The purpose of this meeting is to get you to buy the program we are offering you before we leave this room." Right away the approach rubbed the company head the wrong way because it put the transaction first—before any relationship had been established. Customers who view you as a closing machine will rarely share the kind of information that leads to a good relationship. When a healthy buyer/seller relationship develops, points of common interest develop as well and transactions follow.

5. PUT LOGIC FIRST, THEN EMOTION

When I first meet a client I never assume that we are going to be friends. Before the emotional side of building a relationship develops, I have to establish the rational or functional side. Why should you do business with me if you're already dealing with another supplier? Why should you try us? How are our products different? What unique value do we bring to the table?

I have seen a lot of old-school salespeople get into trouble with young buyers by instinctively jumping into the "let's be friends" approach. Putting the personal side of the relationship first does not always play well with the new generation of buyers, who typically do not have the time their predecessors had to spend on building relationships.

6. EARN THEIR RESPECT FIRST, THEN ADD ENTHUSIASM

Another mistake I see old-style salespeople make is to infuse their early meetings with forced enthusiasm. In today's selling environment, customers are looking for people who are truly helpful and avoid ones that come off as overly enthusiastic zombies. But if you can earn your customer's respect first, the situation changes. An enthusiastic salesperson who is respected has a terrific effect on sales. Earning respect comes from doing just about everything right. Says Jeffrey Zink, eastern regional vice president at Yahoo!, "Credibility comes from really listening to a client's needs and not trying to ram something down their throat. Credibility comes from the fact that you're really interested in their business and how you're going to help them. Credibility is living up to every single obligation and promise you say you will deliver. Credibility is following through on things you say you will take care of. Credibility is resolving all issues they have. Credibility is something you have to earn. It doesn't just automatically come to you."

7. FIND THE MEANING

Some customers are besieged by salespeople wanting to develop close relationships. Barry Nathanson, publisher of *Beverage Aisle*, takes a different approach. "Building a relationship is not about memorizing the names of a client's wife and kids, taking them out to dinner, or getting to know their secretary. These are superficial techniques that every client sees right through. Developing a relationship is about making a client feel special every time I talk to them, by connecting with each client about things that are meaningful to them." Nathanson takes the time to listen and develop an ongoing dialogue with customers about subjects that are meaningful to them as individuals. For some, the dialogue is about the passion they feel for their business; for others, it's their enthusiasm for a sports team, and for others it's about their kids. Nathanson has developed the sensitivity to discover what is meaningful for each individual and the sincerity to pursue that meaning in an ongoing dialogue.

8. FRIENDSHIP AT LAST

If you are able to develop a business friend, you have been given an opportunity to be influential. But as Jim Schroer, vice president of global marketing at Ford, says, "If you want to influence a friend to do something, you do it differently than if it's just a business associate. Maybe you think they're managing their YMCA basketball team wrong. You might think, "I know John pretty well, and if I tell him, he's going to respond negatively or he's not going to accept what I'm saying. But if you're sensitive to how a person ticks, you can explain it in terms that they should be able to understand. You have to handle a conversation as friendly counsel. Look, I'm here as a friend and here are some things you should consider."

Sometimes these friendships develop very naturally. You wake up one morning and during a call to a client you realize you've become friends. When a good client of mine announced his retirement one day, the news made me sad because I had enjoyed his company over the previous five years. I didn't think we were very close, so I was surprised when I received an invitation to his retirement party. I did not realize how popular he was at his company until I arrived at the event and found myself in a huge hall with a fancy catered lunch for over a hundred people gathered in his honor. I also didn't realize how popular I was with him until I was shown to my seat—right next to his at the head table—and introduced as one of his best friends.

Reality Check

What if the client doesn't want a relationship? Every client has more salespeople clamoring for a relationship than she has time to develop. Here are several questions to ask yourself if a client seems to be backing away from you:

1. DO YOU NEED A RELATIONSHIP?

I have had many good buyers who bought lots from me whom I was never friends with. The facts were enough and they were pleased to keep the relationship on a time-efficient, transactional level. Sometimes this is not a bad thing. Clients who are under pressure to produce high-efficiency buying volume truly don't have the time or the desire to develop relationships.

If you can aid them in executing their transactions quickly and smoothly, that will be relationship enough.

2. WHAT IS BLOCKING THE DEVELOPMENT OF A RELATIONSHIP?

If a relationship doesn't develop naturally, for no apparent reason, it's possible that there is something in the way, such as a relationship with a competitor. The client may fear that if he develops a relationship with you, he will have to back out of a relationship with another salesperson when he shifts business in your direction.

3. IS IT ABOUT TIME?

It's best not to take it personally. Sometimes customers just don't have the time to develop relationships. If your product is not a core buy for them it may be a waste for them to invest a lot of time in developing a relationship with you.

Application Question

How can I develop a relationship of influence from a dialogue based on things that are meaningful to each of my customers?

11

Motivating Your Customer by
Creating Value

% of salespeople who have used this approach in the past 12 months:

Not used
21.6%

Used
78.4%

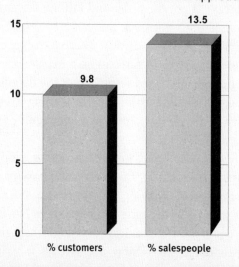

% of customers vs. salespeople
who think this is THE most influential approach

9.8 — % customers

13.5 — % salespeople

"Occasionally you make the kind of call where the customer would pull out a checkbook and pay you for the call because you've done something that really created value for them. The big issue for companies today is how to convert your sales staff from value communicators into value creators."

NEIL RACKHAM, president of Huthwaite, Inc.,
and creator of SPIN Selling

It used to be called "merchandising" and it worked this way: I would start to negotiate an agreement and my client would ask for a lower price. Then I would offer some merchandising: an extra service, a free survey, a free list rental. My client would take this back to his boss, proclaim victory, and say, "Look what I got out of them!" At the same time I could go back to my boss and say, "I got the order and I didn't lower our price." Everyone was happy. But over the years I noticed that about three-quarters of these hard-won merchandising concessions went unclaimed. We would agree to do a market research study for a client, but when I called to work out the details, the client claimed she did not have the time. A free mailing-list rental went unclaimed when the client claimed she just didn't have the time to use the extra service.

Today, there's a smarter, more demanding crop of buyers who understand that many value-added concessions of the past had little value beyond making the buyer and seller look good during transactions. In the past ten years there has been a shift in the way companies strategically manage their resources in competitive markets. These new approaches have opened up possibilities of adding value in ways that would have been unthinkable a decade ago. Jim Morgan, editor emeritus of *Purchasing* magazine wrote, "Companies that once tried to compete largely with their own resources are learning to identify their core competencies and the core competencies of their key suppliers. They then use a mixture of both to compete in the marketplace. Added value as it is used by managers in today's highly competitive environment is about successfully tapping into supplier knowledge, experience, and ideas."

When you create a product or service, you develop expertise in several core areas. The cost of extending this expertise by offering new services or information to your customers is minimal. But if one of your customers were to try and develop these same services, it would cost a fortune because they would first have to develop the core expertise.

The question every sales organization is asking today is this: What core expertise do we possess that can be economically converted into services that our customers would have to spend far more on if they were to develop it themselves? The answer to this question takes on a wide variety of forms depending on your customers and the industry you're in.

What started as the process of throwing an extra bauble into a sales package to speed up an order has evolved into a new style of doing business.

OLD THINKING	Value added is an extra you tack onto the sale to protect a price or to speed up a sale.
WHAT'S DIFFERENT	Customers have realized these "extras" had little real value beyond the transaction. New thinking on how companies compete by leveraging their core competencies has opened up new value-added opportunities that would have been unthinkable ten years ago.

NEW THINKING It's not about extras, it's about expertise. By leveraging your company's internal expertise you can offer at little cost to your organization, related services, information, or advice that would cost your clients big dollars to develop on their own.

Approaches

BUNDLE WITH EXTRA SERVICES

In the mid 1980s a number of my manufacturing clients faced competitive pressures that were reducing their products to commodities. Several fought back by wrapping their product in a service. In bundling their product and service together, the hope was that customers would have trouble telling where one ended and the other began. Today, service companies face the same pressure. At United Parcel Service, vice president of sales Joel Rossman said, "At the end of the day, picking up a package from point A and delivering it to point B is a commodity. We have to do a lot to set ourselves apart from our competition by sharing information on package location, possible delays, and who signed for it."

Again, you're looking to offer a service that your company has the expertise to develop, but that your customers would have to spend a lot of money to create on their own. Consider: An office-furniture supplier offers to design your new office space for free. You sit down with them and explain the square footage of your space, the number of personnel you have, and what activities they will be involved in. The supplier generates an architectural quality layout that makes your entire staff happy. The people who work at this office furniture supply company do nothing all day but think about office furniture.

For them, designing office space is easy. But most companies don't have office planners on staff. Finding someone with that kind of expertise or developing it internally would come at considerable cost.

BECOME CONSULTANTS

Ever since Mack Hanan wrote the classic *Consultative Selling*, salespeople have been challenged to present themselves as consultants seeking to improve their customers' profit. The transformation of the sales organization at Dell Computer holds key lessons.

When Dell Computer was founded in 1984, the sales approach was to offer custom-made computers at factory-direct rock-bottom prices. Dell grew by moving their sales approach beyond low price offerings—they became a consultative sales organization. Says John Kinnaird, vice president and general manager Preferred Account Division at Dell, "We still have great prices, but today we also offer a lot of services as well. My people are trained to help customers buy the things they need to solve a wide variety of technology problems. If you want to set up an Internet site for your company, my people know how to help you do that. We can even help finance the program or lease the entire package." Today, Dell may not sell the cheapest computers, but they have achieved enormous growth by offering value added through sales agents who take a consultative approach.

GET INVOLVED WITH THE CHANNEL OR SUPPLY CHAIN

If there is a way to automate the transactions between your company and your customers, you can add value. According to Kevin Fitzgerald, editor in chief at *Purchasing* magazine, "Buyers today are looking to outsource activities that don't add value and there's no value added by an employee solely devoted to cutting purchase orders. They want to automate transactions. Five years from now, at the most forward-looking companies, purchasing will be out of the business of processing transactions and move into more strategic activities such as managing a global supply base, research and negotiations of long-term contracts with suppliers, and even design and development work."

REPACKAGE INFORMATION

Every time UPS ships a package it generates information. By leveraging the information it collects in the twelve million packages it ships every day, UPS has built a number of services that go beyond delivering packages. According to Joel Rossman, their vice president of sales, "Say we have a customer who wants to open a distribution center somewhere in the continental United States. Where should they look? We have models that can tell them what cities they should consider to deliver from for the best cost and reach for their customer base."

OTHER APPROACHES

How does your company extend its expertise and offer additional value? Here's a list of different approaches I have seen work:

1. Help your customer go global

According to Joel Rossman, UPS uses the information gathered on package delivery to help small businesses considering overseas expansion understand the logistics of their destinations. Says Rossman, "For a small business shipping overseas, we can offer a tremendous amount of information. We understand nuances of the countries you want to ship to, as well as their customs requirements.

2. Access to internal support

If you work for a large company, you may have internal support staff with expertise that is not utilized every business day. Sometimes it's possible to tap into this internal resource and offer a value-added service to a customer who needs it. Marriott's Bruce Himelstein describes one such situation: "One of our major accounts was in the process of adding day care to their corporate headquarters and didn't really know how to do it. We know how to do this really well. We have state-of-the-art child care at our corporate facilities. So we put our human resource folks in touch with them and they are helping them to design a day-care center. This has nothing to do with booking room nights or reservations or market share, it's just about adding value to the relationship."

3. Access to training

Says David Fortanbary, director of cardiovascular marketing for Bristol-Myers Squibb, "I work for a top customer-service organization. A doctor running a medical group maybe has fifteen or twenty or perhaps over 100 physicians in his practice and maybe another thirty or forty staff people. They don't have an internal training department like I do. They don't have access to all of those tools and resources that having a training department gives me. But they do have many of the same issues. We can take some of those folks that are Bristol-Myers Squibb employees and have them do a training program. No matter what the needs of our smaller customers are, we're such a large company that if we look hard enough, we often have someone here who has expertise that a customer can use.

4. Co-management

If you are bundling your product with a lot of services, consider packaging the overall management of your product as well. With this approach you present yourself as a manager of an area of expertise or competency rather than merely as a provider of a specific product. When you do this you are offering to take responsibility for the entire performance of your product area. I know of a dealer organization that does this with great success. Instead of simply being handed a product and representing it, this dealer organization takes on the total product management responsibilities for the entire product, and their compensation package is based on the overall results of their ability to sell it. Along the way, they manage the advertising, promotion and trade-show budgets as well as providing owners with feedback about the future development of the product. This organization works a lot with overseas companies who have no capabilities in the United States. They don't just take on products and sell them, they extend extra services to the point where they are managing the sale of the product in the United States from launch to delivery.

5. Extend financial services

UPS has a division called UPS Capital Corporation. In essence, this group looks at funding aspects of a customer's business. According to Rossman, "If you can enable a client's business to grow more rapidly, everybody benefits."

6. Customization

The ability to present a customized version of your product or service adds value to it. If you can customize to meet the exact needs of a customer, you offer them savings. They're getting precisely what they need but not a lot of extras they don't. These days few products are presented as is, off the shelf. If the physical nature of the product doesn't change, then perhaps there is some customization in the financial or shipping arrangements, the personnel associated with the product, or timetables. Customization does not always have to be as momentous as a product redesign, it just has to be significant to the customer. According to Dean Marsman, vice president of sales at Prince Manufacturing, "The customer always thinks their part is special. It's kind of like one of our kids. Our kids are extremely special to us. They may not be special to someone else. If you ask an engineer about one of his parts, he's pretty passionate about it. It may be something as simple as a windshield-washer-fluid cover, but boy, that's a pretty special part to him." Sometimes making small modifications that don't require an awful lot in terms of time or resources can make a big difference to people who are passionate about the details of their products. Marsman says, "Sun visors are about as close to a commodity as you can get. But when you can do something special that is important to the client, all of a sudden that part becomes extremely special. Just by adding a special print, some kind of control, or a patented light—that plain, same old visor becomes something extremely valuable."

7. Outsource

According to John Kinnaird at Dell Computer, "One way we support our larger customers is to train, employ, and locate dedicated Dell service personnel to man a company's internal help desk. Since we are constantly involved with changing technologies, for us to keep a computer-help-desk person up to speed is no big deal. But for a company in the oil business to do the same would cost them a fortune."

8. Here are some other examples of expertise that can be offered:

- Business consulting for start-up companies

- Free maintenance or technical support

- Free evaluation in your product area. For instance, a utility company could provide energy conservation audits

- Managing a customer's inventory

- Financing the sale of your own products

- Help with shipping logistics, trucking, or storage

- Prepackaging parts together for assembly (also called "kitting" of parts)

- Drop shipment of your products directly from your doorstep to the customer's doorstep

- Help on keeping up with the changing specs of your product when technologies advance

- Help with improving the safe use of your product or service

- Help understanding new processing methods when they come into your market

- Doing the prep work for your product. For instance, many metal manufacturers now offer finishing services

- Insight into where products are headed. For instance, many OEM component manufacturers offer customers product development ideas as to how to improve performance

- Preassembly of components

■ Management of services that you have expertise in. Some service companies that provide maintenance service at manufacturing plants are offering to take over other areas such as ongoing equipment maintenance, janitorial or guard services, even food service

■ Help in recycling product waste

■ Advice to keep your customers competitive in their marketplace

■ Help evaluating the performance your product is offering to your customer

■ Research services that analyze your customer's competitive presence in his marketplace

■ Advice on new product development

Step-by-Step

1. ASK, "WHAT ARE OUR CORE COMPETENCIES?"

As a sales organization, you can offer virtually any service to a customer to induce them to buy your product. But if the service you offer costs exactly what your customer would pay for it on the open market, you have no competitive advantage. The challenge is to offer extra services, information, or expertise that is a matter of extending your own internal expertise so that it really doesn't cost your organization a whole lot of money. The starting point for this kind of analysis is to understand what unique internal expertise you have.

2. LISTEN TO WHAT YOUR CLIENT IS TRYING TO ACCOMPLISH IN YOUR PRODUCT AREA

In most selling situations, the value-added extras that you can offer are not unlike those that your competitors can offer. Often if a competitor finds out about a unique value-added service you are offering, he can duplicate it. The real successes in value-added offers come from understanding a customer well enough to offer a customized package that no one has thought to offer him before.

3. DON'T THINK VALUE ADDED, THINK VALUE *NEEDED*

Says Forest Harper, vice president, Roeing Division at Pfizer, "I reject the conventional idea of value added where you show a client a laundry list of items he or she can choose from. Before we get to that, we understand the client's needs completely. Only then do we talk about value added." Harper's team takes the time to learn the client's needs, then selects the appropriate value-added benefits, and presents them as a package or a program. "Value needed" means putting an understanding of the customer's needs first and putting a package of value-added benefits together for presentation.

4. TALK SPECIFICS

Says Kevin Fitzgerald, editor in chief of *Purchasing* magazine, "Buyers have heard too many salespeople use value added as simply jargon to try and raise prices. A lot of purchasing people are very skeptical about value added because they've been burned in the past. What buyers look for when they hear salespeople talk about value added are the specifics. When they find a salesperson who can document value added, they become very enamored of them because it helps them justify their own operation and performance to their supervisors. It's one thing to say that we've been told this product will reduce operating costs by 20 percent over the next few years. Having some form of documentation makes a big difference."

5. MAKE IT TURNKEY

The object of value added from a buyer's point of view is to tap into supplier resources. But time is often the most valued resource of all, so if you tie up your customer's time resources in the process of delivering other benefits, it often reduces the overall value you are offering. Whatever program you come up with, you ideally want to present it to your client like this: "Sign here and we take care of the rest."

6. KEEP LISTENING

The best value-added programs extend your involvement with a customer. Use value-added programs as opportunities to extend the time you spend with the customer in ways that help you gain a better understanding of their business. For example, a value-added program that helps a customer account for their inventory affords you and your organization access to useful information. This may allow you to propose new ways to work together or to develop new products or services.

7. REMEMBER WHAT YOU'RE SELLING

I have seen salespeople so enamored of the value-added services they have to offer that they forget to sell the core product! Sometimes value-added services add sizzle and interest to commodity sales. They may well be more interesting to talk about than the actual product. Remember that without the sale of the central product you are offering, these value-added services could not exist.

Reality Check

WHAT IF MY COMPETITION OFFERS THE SAME VALUE-ADDED SERVICES?

Value-added extras that become widely used can become commodities. The first airline to issue frequent-flier miles gained a short-term advantage, but in time, every airline started up its own frequent-flier program and the benefit became a commodity.

Real value added comes from customer understanding and the unique application of value-added services. If you don't understand your customer or his needs, chances are you won't be able to develop services of unique value to him. The key is to present value added in ways that uniquely help a client achieve their goals.

Application Question

How can we leverage our in-house expertise into services or information that have dollar value to our customers?

12

Motivating Your Customer by
Partnering

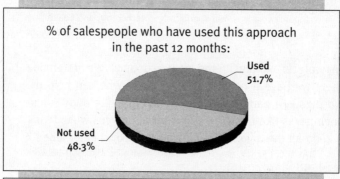

% of salespeople who have used this approach in the past 12 months:

Used 51.7%

Not used 48.3%

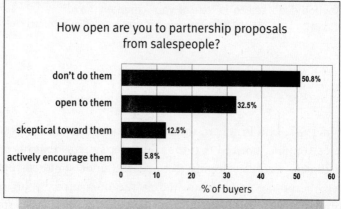

How open are you to partnership proposals from salespeople?

don't do them — 50.8%
open to them — 32.5%
skeptical toward them — 12.5%
actively encourage them — 5.8%

% of buyers

"New product announcements aren't nearly as important anymore. Everybody assumes you have technology. We're at a point where technology isn't even that important. Everyone assumes you have technology. Now, it's all about business models. And what really validates your business model are your partners and your customers."

JESSE D. ODELL, account supervisor at Schwartz Communications, a public relations firm specializing in technology and health-care companies (as quoted in *BusinessWeek*, October 25, 1999)

"My role is unique in the new economy. We determine where we have a need, find the people who can help us, and pursue a partnership. Selling to several groups simultaneously is like being a ringmaster at a circus while trying to keep all the animals in line and the crowd entertained."

DAVID C. CAFFEY, director of development, The Microsoft Network

"Anybody you sell to is part of your company now."

LEE IACOCCA, chairman and founder, EV Global Motors

In 1987, Lou Pritchett, then vice president of sales at Procter & Gamble, noticed that the computer systems that his retail customers were developing to track and understand customers were becoming as sophisticated as the ones used by his own company. Pritchett also noticed that his company's systems were not coordinated in any way with these retailers. It seemed to him there was an opportunity to integrate the systems to improve efficiency for both parties. But integrating these systems meant sharing sensitive data and cooperating in ways that buyers and sellers had never done before.

Pritchett's first attempt to sell his idea of cooperation failed as the management at Kmart turned him down flat. He then fixed his sights on Wal-Mart and called a mutual friend, George Billingsley, to arrange a business meeting with Sam Walton, Wal-Mart's founder and principal owner. Billingsley told Pritchett that Walton was not a "corporate type"; in fact, he hated formality. He told Pritchett not to try to sell Sam Walton "through the front door" and instead set up an unconventional meeting where Pritchett met Walton on a canoe trip down the South Fork of the Spring River in Hardy, Arkansas. It became the unlikely meeting place where the first large-scale partnering agreement in business history began.

Pritchett told Walton he was absolutely convinced that by planning together and joining their systems they could both achieve a competitive advantage by reducing costs. As Walton started to see the possibilities he said, "Just think, Lou, what we could do if we could think of each other as extensions of one another's operations! Procter would see that my stores are their stores and that what we are doing is going to affect your product on the shelf."

Today, this collaborative approach enjoys wide acceptance. The October 25, 1999, issue of *BusinessWeek* states, "According to Andersen Consulting, alliances will represent $25 trillion to $40 trillion in value within the next five years. The firm concludes that the average large company, which had no alliances a decade ago, now has in excess of 30."

Pritchett insists that the underlying star in the Wal-Mart/ Procter & Gamble partnership was new enabling technology. He says, "Partnering is really about taking two unconnected, incompatible systems and joining them together so they become one system and one organization becomes an extension of the other." Pritchett's partnership involved joining retail information systems, but today, partnering encompasses product development systems, customer-service systems, brand management systems, distribution systems, and technology development systems.

The goal in partnering with another company is to accomplish something together that neither company could accomplish alone. As technologies, customer access, loyal customer bases and brands become more expensive to build from scratch, companies are making strategic alliances to borrow what they need and get to where they need to go faster.

OLD THINKING	To successfully compete for customers, rely on internal resources so you can maintain total control.
WHAT'S DIFFERENT	Companies now compete with a powerful combination of their resources and resources from complementary companies. We are evolving from a climate in which stand-alone companies compete with each other to a climate in which groups of compatible companies compete with other groups.
NEW THINKING	Partnering is a way to move faster into competitive markets and capture more customers. Salespeople are often in a position to understand where partnerships can help, and are often empowered to initiate them.

Approaches

INITIATE A PARTNERSHIP WITH AN ALLIED COMPANY

"It's the field salesman who's probably going to realize what the customer wants, and what others are offering that might complement it," says Michael Brinkman, director of strategic business development, Panasonic Broadcast & Digital Systems Company. Smart companies listen to partnership ideas from their sales staff, who are often in the best position to spot the opportunities.

Often it's management's job to take over and develop the partnership ideas, but even that is changing. I interviewed several salespeople whose sole job is to "sell" the idea of partnering with the company they represent. This new breed of salesperson comes to the table empowered to initiate and develop partnerships.

FORM A PERSONAL PARTNERSHIP WITH A CUSTOMER

Partnerships aren't limited to deals done on a corporate scale. It only takes two people to form a partnership. In the 1950s a young Lou Pritchett was a Procter & Gamble field manager who initiated a partnership with a buyer at a large wholesaler. Pritchett asked himself what he could do to make this buyer think of him as an extension of his own business. He recalls, "I convinced this wholesaler to let me visit his company every week, take inventory for my own products, and write up my own orders." In those days giving a salesperson the power to write up his own orders was like putting a fox in the henhouse. But, says Pritchett, "Maybe I could write up a carload of extra business but I would only get to do it once." The result of this extra effort paid off as the customer began to view Pritchett as a de facto member of his organization. He says, "I was as well known to the warehouse manager as any member of the staff." This relationship gave Pritchett access to internal company information as well as a big edge over his competition.

TARGET ANOTHER SALESPERSON WHO SELLS AN ALLIED PRODUCT

I once had a client who sold professional camera batteries who formed a personal partnership with a sales rep from a camera manufacturer. Before televison cameras wear out, the batteries that power them typically need replacement. The battery salesperson could then tip off the camera salesperson that a station might need to replace their cameras soon. And when a station places a large camera order they often order extra backup batteries at the same time, so the camera salesperson could refer business back to the battery salesperson. These two had an informal arrangement that worked for their mutual benefit.

This arrangement was never officially sanctioned by either company and could never have become corporate policy. No battery company could ever partner with one camera company on a corporate level for fear of alienating the other camera makers. But when the partnership was kept on a personal level, the individuals benefited.

INITIATE A PARTNERSHIP WITH A COMPETITOR

There are times when partnering with your competition makes sense if you are trying to build up a product category, platform, or technical standard. Says Panasonic's Michael Brinkman, "If you have 100 percent of the market for a product, format, or service that's not widely used, you don't make nearly as much money as if you have a slice of the market for something that has wide acceptance." Brinkman advocates a combination of cooperating and competing. "First you all work hard together to make the pie bigger, then you compete to get your slice." Brinkman does not find this model of "coopetition" incompatible with human nature. He went on to describe how professional cyclists both compete and cooperate during a race. "Bicycle racers can go faster when they are part of a pack of five or six racers. So they cooperate to go faster until they get to near the finish line and then they break apart and speed like mad to win."

Partnering with your competition can be hard on salespeople. I was at a company's trade-show booth where a competitor/partner's product was being displayed alongside the company's offerings. I watched with amusement as a salesperson giving a visitor a tour damned the competitor's product with very faint praise.

Brinkman, who successfully initiated the "coopetition" model among the DVC Pro Users Group, says that it can be very difficult to implement because companies actually have to help their competition win. "For many companies it requires a massive adjustment." How many people on your sales staff are ready to encourage a customer to use a competitor's product?

Step-by-Step

1. RECOGNIZE PARTNERING OPPORTUNITIES

As you cover your territory, be sensitive to opportunities that might benefit your company. The question to ask yourself is: Whom can we work with to capture more customers or reduce costs?

Here are some partnership benefits that I have seen in action:

- Co-development of technology
- Mutual access to customer base

- Elimination of transaction costs

- Establishing a new standard

- Borrow credibility

- Category growth

- Shared expertise

- Shared risk

- Reduced risk

- Extension of a brand's umbrella

- Global Competitiveness

- Equal footing with much larger companies (by forming a group of smaller ones)

2. EVALUATING PARTNERING PROSPECTS

When Robin Blunt, vice president international sales, Global Marketing Programs at MasterCard, initiates contact for a potential partnership, he likes to start with a referral or introduction of some kind. Says Blunt, "I look at the different categories of companies I want to form partnerships with and look for companies who are already friendly with my organization. I network out to these people and say, 'We're already working together, but I'd like to take that to the next level, what do you think?' "

3. APPROACH AT THE RIGHT LEVEL

Bill Etherington, senior and group executive, sales and distribution at IBM, says that partnering is not likely to work unless you approach the organization at a high enough level.

He says, "You have to call on the decision maker—the CEO, CFO, or the CIO—because partnership implies softer values that are best discussed at this level. The purchasing department is the wrong place to start these discussions—they love to see as many bidders as possible at the lowest price and highest value."

4. START A DIALOGUE

"Partnering can involve a lot of change, so it's best to start slowly," says MasterCard's Robin Blunt. "You don't want to scare somebody off by proposing a fully integrated, comprehensive marketing partnership right away. First we find an area where we can nurture some level of trust. We start with something simple, then have a platform to go on to the next level."

Says David Caffey, director of business development at The Microsoft Network, "We start by trying to find out what both companies' goals are. Then we see if we can map out a way to help them achieve goals other than what the initial negotiation had started out with."

5. BE FLEXIBLE

Often a partnership dialogue can extend into areas you may not have considered. David Caffey says, "When we initiate a partnership relationship, we never know where it's going to end up. We try to expand the synergies that our two organizations have and typically start out talking about a relatively small transaction and then end up involved with a much greater arrangement. It really comes down to playing off the core competencies of the partners. What I then try to do is to drive a deal to its *illogical* conclusion."

6. STAFF THE DIALOGUE

In the euphoria of possibilities that can come out of these meetings, it is important to remember that partnering requires investment. Says Alec Shapiro, vice president of marketing communications, at Sony Broadcast & Professional Company, "Too often companies say they want to partner with other companies but they don't dedicate any personnel or financial resources to make that happen. Partnership doesn't just happen through osmosis or having a few good meetings."

Often it is hard for companies to allocate resources since no one really knows what the financial return will be. But investment is required to fuel an ongoing process. Says Shapiro, "Having partners is hard. You can't just mail your specs out and hope that your partners pick up and run with them. Every partnership has a separate, ongoing dialogue that needs attention."

7. THE INTERNAL PART OF THE SELL

For the salesperson initiating a partnership, very often there is as much selling that needs to be done inside her own company as to the prospective partner. Sometimes partnerships mean a shifting of control or responsibilities and that kind of change is difficult. According to Lou Pritchett, "When you sell your partnership idea internally you need to look at the reward and recognition system that is in place at your company. Sometimes shifting some of the buying power to a customer shifts it away from a manager's turf. Change agents should never sacrifice themselves in the field of battle. Remember you have to live to fight another day."

8. THE NEXT LEVEL

Robin Blunt of MasterCard says that when you finally get past the preliminaries and move on to discussing how the partnership can blossom, it gets very exciting. According to Blunt, "This is where it really becomes magical. You can start to free-associate a bit and truly innovate. 'Hey, remember that idea that you had two years ago? How about bringing in another party and taking it to the next level?' And your partner says, 'I like your thinking, that sounds great!' "

9. MEASURE THE RESULTS

Partnerships are made in order to capture more business or reduce costs. Either activity can be measured. Partnerships can fail when one side doesn't see measurable results. The time to prevent these misunderstandings is at the beginning of the partnership deal. A key question at that initial stage is: How do we measure results? Partnerships might mean you need to share sensitive data on sales or cost savings.

Reality Check

WHAT IF THE COMPANY YOU WANT TO PARTNER WITH IS PARTNERED WITH A COMPETITOR?

1. Watch for the quiet death

Partnerships, as opposed to acquisitions, can be undone very quickly. Most partnerships are announced with much fanfare, but when they die they typically go away very quietly. If you're interested in a partnership with an already partnered company, monitor the health of that partnership. You may be able to move in if enthusiasm flags or either side drops the ball.

2. Make a noncompeting overture in another area

Depending on the nature of your business, it may be possible to partner with the same company and start working together in a different capacity.

Application Question

How can we share our core competencies with other companies to capture more customers or reduce costs?

13

Motivating Your Customer by
Selling a System

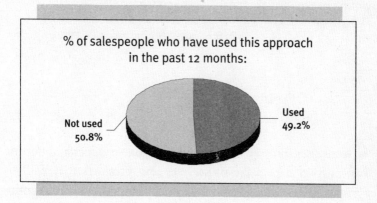

% of salespeople who have used this approach in the past 12 months:

Not used
50.8%

Used
49.2%

"If the customer wants no more than to replace worn-out equipment, there's just so much you can do. But if a customer is willing to consider a process change, you can bring them far more benefit. Since 'process change' involves the word 'change' it makes many customers nervous."

CONRAD COFFIELD, vice president, broadcast & production sales,
Sony Broadcast and Professional Company

S omeone, somewhere is looking at your product and putting together a package of services and products that will supersede your selling efforts. If he or she is successful, your entire product category will be reduced to a component of their package. You could end up with very little say about whether your product or a competitor's is included.

While the most widely publicized examples of this are in the computer and information technology areas, this kind of strategic thinking is happening in every industry.

Today companies frequently outplace entire billing systems, security systems, maintenance systems, product engineering, distribution, and component manufacturing. Less commonly, I have seen marketing and personnel functions outplaced as well.

As more companies focus their resources on their core competencies and outplace nonstrategic functions, system selling will continue to grow.

OLD THINKING Stay focused on selling your product, consider everyone else a competitor.

WHAT'S DIFFERENT In the networked economy, there are no stand-alone products or services. Your products will be included in system-level proposals with or without your help.

- -

NEW THINKING If you don't sell your products on a system level, someone else will do it for you.

Approaches

REDESIGN A CUSTOMER SYSTEM

With advances in technology it is often possible to redesign how your customer does business in your product area. The result can be huge increases in productivity. Joe Valenti, senior vice president at Xerox Business Services, imagines how his organization would approach a bank customer: "We can sell a bank a printer that can print statements twice as fast, but we can offer much greater productivity if we redesign their entire system. To do this we need to find out how information is developed, transmitted, and stored at their company. Then we can propose a system redesign that eliminates steps in work flow and consolidates others. Doing this, we can often double the speed of the entire process of creating bank statements, not just their printing."

A salesperson who can spearhead the redesign of an entire system for a bank is going to sell a lot more product than one who just sells that bank a new printer.

PARTICIPATE IN A LARGER SYSTEM INVOLVING SEVERAL SUPPLIERS

Often system-level solutions require that several suppliers work together. This puts salespeople in a new position; they take the point and lead a system proposal, or work with another company's sales team that is taking the lead. This calls for an unusual degree of cooperation between salespeople from different companies. Says Frank Pinto vice president of worldwide sales at Sun Microsystems, "In this kind of environment the individual salesperson can't do it alone anymore. That lone gunslinger has got to become a team leader and bring in the right partners to help solve the customer's problem. This is a unique skill set and we spend a lot of time training salespeople to work this way."

SELL THROUGH A SYSTEM INTEGRATOR

In many markets there are companies that build customized packages using the products of various suppliers. The key to selling through system integrators is to plan ahead and treat these integrators like your best customers or dealers.

When a system integrator needs a product in your category, she typically goes to a supplier they have a relationship with. If you have done your homework and spent some time developing a relationship with her, chances are you'll be on her list. But once the integrator gets an order to build a system, it is often too late for a sales call. She is going to move forward immediately with a supplier she already knows and trusts.

Selling to system integrators means investing time and building relationships before the order comes in. Many system integrators regularly meet with suppliers to learn what they can offer. I know a system integration company that holds meetings with suppliers every month. These meetings are educational in nature and not a place for hard-driving sales pitches.

Selling to system integrators may require a different style of customer service than your company customarily offers. Clients don't really need a lot of hand-holding, but when they need product information, they need detailed information and they need it instantly.

SELL THE SYSTEMS BEHIND YOUR BRAND

When you sell a client into a long-term contract, your organizations work together over the long haul. It is often the quality of your internal systems that determine the quality of the relationship after the sale. I once worked for a company that had terrible customer-service, credit, and collection systems, which made keeping long-term clients very difficult.

Smart buyers are often interested in the quality of the systems you have in place. If your systems are antiquated and inefficient, interfacing with them can be a drain on the systems of the client company. By contrast, if your company develops a reputation for its great systems, it can help you win new business and keep it. Says Gregg Hammann, vice president, national accounts at Coca-Cola, "It's not just our brand that makes companies want to do business with us, it's the whole Coca-Cola business system. It's our corporate infrastructure, delivery systems, and marketing systems. We help companies build their business by leveraging our business system."

Step-by-Step

1. ASK YOURSELF, "FROM MY CUSTOMER'S POINT OF VIEW, WHICH SYSTEM(S) ARE MY PRODUCTS A PART OF?"

Every product and service you sell is a component of several of your customer's larger systems: payment and collection systems, customer-service systems, new product development systems, product management systems, pricing systems, fulfillment systems, delivery systems, order-taking systems, marketing systems, lead fulfillment systems, maintenance systems and customer feedback systems, to mention just a few. Look at how your product is used within this context. Is it part of a greater function, system, or department that can be entirely outplaced?

2. ASK, "HOW COULD WE PROVIDE A SYSTEM-LEVEL SOLUTION?"

If your company is not set up to handle a system-level solution, think about how you could offer one. Are there other companies you can cooperate with? Are they companies your organization could buy?

3. ASK, "WHEN DOES THE CUSTOMER'S ANNUAL BUDGET BEGIN?"

A major system-level sale is not typically purchased with everyday cash flow. Often the buyer writes the sale as a major expense into next year's capital budget. If your client's annual budget begins on January 1, plan to start your selling efforts many months before that date.

4. TALK ABOUT ROI

Often system-level sales are made by mapping out ROI (return on investment) over time. The ROI sales story sounds like this: "If you install this system, you will cut your expenses by 25 percent per year. In four years the system will pay for itself and then go on to generate the same savings annually." Often it is a numbers sell based on costs saved or potential new revenue generated over time.

5. TALK ABOUT THE ADVANTAGES OF ONE POINT OF CONTACT

Another major benefit of the system-level sale is that one person or company becomes responsible for making the different components provided by different companies work together. When one company oversees the entire project the client has to deal with only one point of contact. Typically, systems fail because components provided by different suppliers are incompatable. With one point of contact the client's job becomes much simpler.

6. FIND THE DECISION MAKER

Often half of the challenge of selling a system is to find the individual or committee who can actually make a decision this big.

If you are proposing a system that involves several departments, you may have to sell to several groups simultaneously. Alternately you can sell to the person they all report to. Typically a major system sale needs to be signed off by someone very high in the organization.

7. REDUCE THE PERCEPTION OF RISK

While there are many upsides to consolidating functions into a larger system, there is one huge downside. If that larger system fails, it takes a big chunk of the company's functionality down with it. You cannot sweep this concern under a rug.

Be honest about the risks and straightforward about how problems can be dealt with. If possible, cite situations where your company has successfully handled sticky situations. You can also point out the competitive risk of not moving toward a system solution if others in your customer's market are going that route. Says Larry Wilson, author of *Stop Selling, Start Partnering*, "Look at the business you're in. Are the companies that are not changing prospering and moving ahead? No! The companies that are hanging on the way they've always done things are going to be the best player in a game that's no longer being played."

Reality Check

WHAT IF YOU ARE NOT INCLUDED IN A SYSTEM PROPOSAL THAT HAS BEEN ACCEPTED?

Typically system integrators propose a package but will change suppliers if the end user wants a specific brand included in the package. If you have a relationship with the end user, you can call on them to see if you can be put back into the proposal before the system is built.

The second thing you need to do is to take a long-term approach toward building a relationship with the system integrator. If you don't, chances are good they will use someone else's product in the next system they build.

Application Question

How can we offer a system-level sell that encompasses many products and services to solve a bigger client problem?

14

Motivating Your Customer by
Creating Experiences

% of salespeople who have used this approach in the past 12 months:

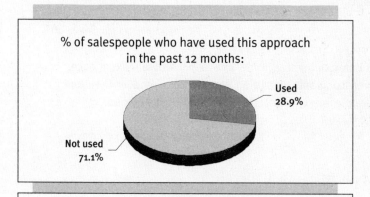

Used
28.9%

Not used
71.1%

% of salespeople using this approach vs. % of customers who report being influenced by it in the last 12 months

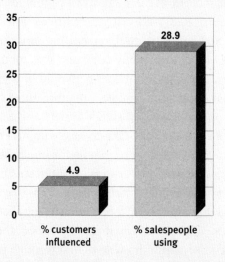

"The experience of doing business with our company is more than the product. The whole experience includes the meeting with an agent as well as his education, professionalism, and integrity. Initially, the experience of the meeting is more important to the consumer than the underlying product."

BILL BECKLEY, executive vice president of agencies,
Northwestern Mutual Life

". . . entertainment is only one aspect of an experience. Rather, companies stage an experience whenever they *engage* customers, connecting with them in a personal, memorable way."

B. JOSEPH PINE II and JAMES H. GILMORE, *The Experience Economy*

As a skeptical client of mine sat down to join me for lunch, he looked irritated. "Why are there three extra seats here, Josh?" You're not going to double-team me, are you?" I explained that no one else from my company was joining us but that I had invited some guests whom he would find interesting.

This particular client was a midsize manufacturer of lighting products who sold exclusively through dealers and distributors. As a result, he rarely spent time face-to-face with his end users; I had arranged for three of them to join us for lunch. When I explained, my client nodded his head with interest. On cue, the three joined us. I had scripted a series of questions to get the conversation started, but after the first few minutes my client jumped in with questions of his own. The more he probed, the more he realized that the information flowing to him through his distributors was both limited in scope, and limiting to his business.

My client was moved by the experience, which made him realize he had a communication problem with his end-user customers. Buying advertising space from me helped solve the problem.

No one watching that lunch would have guessed I was selling anything to anyone. I presented no information, showed no price sheets, and overcame no objections. What I did do was create an experience for my customer that helped him discover for himself that he had a need for my product. While conversation flowed freely and casually, the event was a carefully planned one intended to result in a sale.

The Internet has raised customer expectations. With the click of a mouse any customer can contact a company and have an interactive, personalized experience. When you call on a customer in person, you can offer nothing less.

I find my best sales calls are the ones where "something happens," calls during which a client and I together discover, create, experience, discuss, learn, or reject any number of ideas. But if all you do is show up and present product information, you have wasted an opportunity and you could eventually be replaced by a Web site.

OLD THINKING	Present your product information and ask for the order. If they don't buy, move to the next customer and start all over again.
WHAT'S DIFFERENT	The Internet is training customers to expect an interactive, customized experience.
NEW THINKING	Presenting information is not enough. Your customers need to experience what you are trying to sell them through doing, feeling, and interacting.

Approaches

ELEVATE A SALES CALL TO AN EVENT

Skilled trainers tell us that people learn better by doing than by listening to lectures. Why is it, then, that in selling the most commonly used method to "teach" clients about our new products and opportunities is to give them a lecture?

To give them an experience you need to *do something* beyond presenting information that makes the visit memorable and personable. Some examples:

Shoot it out

Live product comparisons can be great theater; they're the stuff that experiences are made of. Jodi Stern, Marketing Director for Vin Divino, has a wine buyer to whom she sells routinely by staging a blind taste test. Says Stern, "If I want her to buy my Pino Grigio, I don't say to her, 'This is a Pino Grigio, here, taste it.' Instead I take the Pino Grigio I want her to consider, have her bring the Pino Grigio she's using now from behind the bar, and pour them in unmarked, numbered glasses for her to taste blind. I've done this with her numerous times and the wine she chooses is the wine she buys."

Invite a friend

Bringing special people to a visit can create an experience. Ann Belle Rosenberg, marketing manager for Video Systems, made a fabulous impression on a good client when she invited a second client along on a call. Ann Belle knew they shared interests and guessed correctly that these two could be friends. The two clients did hit it off and that lunch will always be remembered by both as the time when Ann Belle introduced them.

Pick a special setting

At a trade show in Amsterdam I used the location to create memorable events with my American clients. In the course of three days I took one client on a boat ride through the canals, took another client of Dutch-American descent out to dinner at a traditional Dutch restaurant, and had lunch with a third client at a restaurant in a windmill. I conducted business as usual during all three events but used the location to elevate the encounter to an experience.

MAKE ROUTINE CONTACT A MEMORABLE EXPERIENCE

Sidney Friedman, president, Corporate Financial Services, has built a career out of transforming ordinary customer contact into an experience. Says Friedman, "First find out what the whole world is doing and then don't do that. I try to make everything in my life a little different, I 'Sidneyize' it and use it to make a statement."

Some of Friedman's innovations:

On answering phones

"I have three people with English accents answer my phones. They were hired specifically because they've got British accents. Their voices make an impression every time they answer the phone."

On making an entrance

"When I started out in business I bought a white Rolls-Royce and staffed it with a very, very attractive lady chauffeur. You can imagine me coming down the street in the back of a car with a pretty lady opening the door for me. When she picked up clients and took them to my office for appointments, it made quite an impression."

On remembering birthdays

"Anyone can send a birthday card, but if you live here in the Philadelphia area we send you a birthday cake which my driver delivers."

On business cards

"My business card has a picture of me on it, a toll-free phone number, and says simply 'anytime.' "

DELIVER THE RIGHT BUYING EXPERIENCE

Though product designers and engineers would hate to hear it, for many clients the product they buy means less than the personal experience they have during the buying process. The way you and a client interact during a sale creates an experience. I had a client who would not buy from me unless he felt that in doing so, he would end up the big winner. He did not ask about quality or any of the features most buyers asked about, but would instead relentlessly wrestle some kind of concession from me. I once tried to offer a concession up front to prevent the usual struggle. He ignored my attempt to cut short our usual interaction and began pushing for another. I had missed the point. He liked the struggle and the whole experience of a hard-won concession. Without the experience of the "big win," no sale.

I had another client who bought on quality and expected a quality buying experience. Once she told me she had stopped buying from a competitor whose representative she found rude. That in itself may not be unusual. What is remarkable is that though she placed an order with me, she quite frankly told me she felt the quality of this competitor's products was superior to what I was offering. She ranked the quality of the buying experience more important than the quality of the products.

It is worth asking what kind of buying experience your customer wants most.

DEVELOP A CUSTOMER-SERVICE STYLE

Incremental improvements in customer service often go unnoticed, but by consistently delivering a unique style of customer service, you will stand out from the crowd. The challenge is to develop a type of service that makes the experience of dealing with your company different in a way that supports your brand. Richard Sweet, senior director of marketing and sales at Southwest Airlines, understands that his customers get great prices but not all the amenities full-fare carriers offer. Southwest tries to make up for this by creating a style of service that involves a personal, fun feel. Says Sweet, "We encourage our flight attendants to tell jokes, sing songs, and do things that are out of the ordinary. Our ticket and gate agents have the freedom to play games and interact with customers in a jovial, fun-loving way that people remember."

USE EVENT EXPERIENCES AS VALUE ADDED

If you have a leading product in a category, then often you have a market presence that can be leveraged into sponsoring events to include your customers. Rance Crain, president and editorial director of Crain Communications, has found that staging events or experiences around his magazine brands is great value added. Says Crain, "We've found, much to my surprise, that as much as our advertisers want to buy ad space in our publications, they want to use publications, like *Ad Age*, to help sponsor special events that bring them face-to-face with their best customers."

LET THEM EXPERIENCE THE PRODUCT

With simple, inexpensive products this amounts to sampling. Arranging a way to experience a complex product can be challenging. Bruce Lazenby, president and CEO of FreeBalance, wants every potential customer for his government accounting software to have the experience of using it. His company now gives away the base product that used to sell for $52,500. Says Lazenby, "We simply ship the software on a CD and customers can start using it. This approach reduces their risk to zero and gets by the whole government low-bid procurement process. If they like our software and start using it, we can work together on upgrades, additional modules, or adding more users to their system."

CREATE AN EVANGELICAL EXPERIENCE

Adding meaningful enthusiasm to the selling process can transform a call into an experience. But your enthusiasm must be fueled by more than potential commission. Guy Kawasaki, in his book *Selling the Dream*, says that evangelical selling has a lot to do with explaining a product in a way that adds ethical meaning. Says Kawasaki, "Anything can be evangelized. It doesn't have to only be hot, cool technology, or digital stuff. It has to be something that takes the moral high ground, and makes people's lives better. An evangelistic cause is in the eye of the beholder. You could evangelize salt if you got really excited about it."

Step-by-Step

1. CREATING LEARNING EXPERIENCES

Typically, clients do not learn specific product facts from these experiences. Rather, they help customers understand the softer aspects of the sale, such as trust or quality.

When you stage a learning experience you are not teaching your clients, but rather helping them learn for themselves. Creating experiences is an imaginative process in which customers discover on their own the value of what you have to offer. You're not manipulating them since your customers experience the situation on their own terms and draw their own conclusions.

2. SHOW, DON'T TELL

The elements of experience-based learning are not flip charts, presentations, research, or facts; they are interacting, feeling, touching, sensing, and observing. In other words, learning by doing not by listening.

Contrast the difference between telling your customers the following sales messages and staging an experience that makes the message come alive.

Sales message: "We take extra care in quality"

Explaining: "Here is how we check the details. We have aggressive quality control and here is a list of 29 quality checks we make before we ship the product."

Experiencing: In 1985, a European manufacturer of photo products wanted to help magazine editors in the photo industry understand the quality of their organization. My wife, Lynn, editor of *Industrial Photography* magazine at the time, was invited on a weeklong trip to France and England that included numerous plant tours as well as sightseeing trips. One of the highlights of the trip was a dinner in Lyons, France, at the restaurant of one of the greatest chefs on earth, Paul Bocuse. Fifteen years later my wife still counts that dinner among the best of her life. The manufacter communicated their quality by delivering a quality experience.

Sales message: "We care about our customers"

Explaining: "At our company the customer comes first. We're the proud recipients of several customer-service awards."

Experiencing: A client of mine who happens to be a fanatical *Star Trek* fan got a call from a salesperson just before a new *Star Trek* movie was scheduled to open. The salesperson said, "The next *Star Trek* movie opens on Monday and I have two tickets to the three P.M. show. Can you come?" When I visited that client two weeks later she was still talking about it. This salesperson communicated a sense of caring by creating an experience that had personal meaning for the customer.

Sales message: "We offer better quality"

Explaining: "We have the best products. We have more features that offer you these benefits than any of our competitors can."

Experiencing: I once sold ad space against a schlock trade magazine that spent little money on its editorial content and even less on illustrating text with graphics or color of any kind. Since my clients rarely read the magazines they ran ads in, and since there were lots of full-color ads in the magazine, none of my clients had noticed the poor editorial presentation. I took the current issues of my magazine and my competitor's and covered all the ads with sheets of white paper. Without the full-color ads my magazine's editorial still looked great, while my competitor's looked lifeless and dull. I brought out both magazines during my next few calls and explained what I had done as I flipped the pages. Seeing was believing. By visually dramatizing the differences between my product and the competition's, my clients could experience the quality difference for themselves.

3. SCRIPTING THE LEARNING EXPERIENCE

Experiences do not happen by accident. Although they often appear spontaneous to the customer, careful planning is essential. You really do need to think through the sequence of events and script them. If appropriate, rehearse your lines or even the whole event.

4. THEME THE EXPERIENCE

During a family trip to Disney World I learned the power of theming an experience. My daughters, Laura and Jenny, then nine and five, couldn't get enough of the Flying Dumbo ride. The ride is wonderfully designed and adorned with the characters from the classic Disney movie. I groaned as we began yet another forty-five-minute wait for a ride that ended a mere ninety seconds later, accompanied by Laura and Jenny's enthusiastic cries of, "Again! Again!" Months later, back at a Brooklyn amusement park, I spotted an attraction that duplicated the Dumbo ride. Same deal, I thought, you climb into a large box disguised as an animal, whiz around in a circle, and control the box's up-and-down motion with a lever. I enthusiastically pointed out that this ride could do everything the Dumbo ride could do—without the forty-five-minute wait. My kids were not even slightly interested. The Dumbo theme and the beautiful design had created a unique experience that a simple amusement-park ride could not match.

5. MAKE IT PERSONAL

My colleague Ann Belle Rosenberg of Video Systems and I had a tradition of taking two clients out to lunch at an annual trade show in Las Vegas. But this year was different. One of the clients was home recovering from double hip replacement surgery and could not join us. As typical, Rosenberg arranged for a terrific lunch location at the newly opened Venetian hotel overlooking the hotel's theme canal. When drinks arrived she proposed a toast to our friend who could not join us that year.

After lunch, she bought a postcard at a gift shop and wrote a note to our absent comrade mentioning that we had toasted him and looked forward to seeing him next year. We all signed the card and dropped it in the mail. Ann Belle had transformed a simple lunch into an event that honored a friendship. I heard later that the arrival of that postcard at the bedside of our recovering client was also an event. When I asked Rosenberg how she thought of doing it, she replied, "Josh, I always carry stamps in my purse, and remembering Jim was just being considerate."

6. STAGE SURPRISES

I was bone tired as I rolled into the Holiday Inn in Kitchener, Ontario, at 11:05 P.M. My guaranteed room was waiting but I wilted when I heard that the hotel restaurant had closed minutes ago. The receptionist told me about a restaurant a block away that was still open, but I confessed that given the lateness of the hour I had no interest in a dining adventure. All I wanted, I explained, was a sandwich and a good night's sleep. To my amazement she said, "A sandwich? Oh, I can make you a sandwich." I blinked. Had I heard this right? The receptionist at a Holiday Inn was going to make me a turkey-and-tomato sandwich?

The sandwich was in fact promptly delivered to my room and no sandwich has ever tasted so good. It was a small favor but was delivered at a time that made a huge impact on the quality of my stay. The next morning I began to take notice of many small things the hotel staff had done to make my experience better. A routine stay turned into a memorable one for the cost of a turkey sandwich. I doubt that the Holiday Inn in Kitchener had a specific master plan for weary, hungry late arrivals, but clearly they encouraged their staff to be sensitive to customers' needs and had granted them the opportunity to be spontaneous.

Simple acts can make a big impact when they are done at the right moment.

7. LEAVE A MEMENTO

Experiences can have a longer-term impact if you leave something behind as a reminder. Bring your camera and take a picture or buy a souvenir and give it to your customer as a keepsake to remind her of the experience.

Reality Check

WHAT IF YOUR CLIENT DOES NOT WANT TO PARTICIPATE IN YOUR CAREFULLY PLANNED EXPERIENCE?

Experiences require customer participation. Not everyone can leave work and family behind to take a trip to Europe, take two hours off from work to see a new *Star Trek* movie, or even have the motivation to be walked through a pasted up magazine comparison.

Skeptical customers might be quick to turn these out-of-the-ordinary activities down. If the client views the experience you are proposing as manipulative, chances are they'll decline.

I often find that I have to sell the idea of participation. If you sense the customer is avoiding the situation for fear your plan is to manipulate them, say, "Here is what will happen. You may learn something you didn't know before, but in any case you will draw your own conclusions."

Application Question

How can I communicate the value of what I have to offer by creating a personal and memorable experience?

15

Motivating Your Customer by
Competitive Positioning

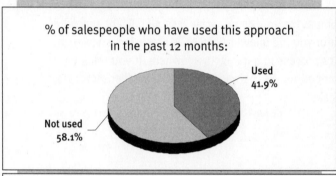

% of salespeople who have used this approach
in the past 12 months:

Used
41.9%

Not used
58.1%

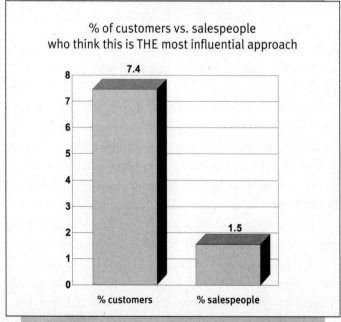

% of customers vs. salespeople
who think this is THE most influential approach

% customers   % salespeople

"Arguments are never made in a vacuum. There are always competitors trying to make arguments of their own. A marketer's message has to make sense in the context of the category. It has to start with what the marketplace has heard and registered from the competition."

JACK TROUT, *Differentiate or Die*

"The competitor you know is far less significant than the competitor you are unaware of who is preparing a new technology or process in a garage somewhere. If you think your only competition is people who make similar products, think again."

GERHARD GSCHWANDTNER, publisher, *Selling Power*

I recently got a call from an old account, one I had not called on in ten years. Back when this company was buying in my market, I remembered how much I enjoyed visiting them. They always took pride in making good buying decisions, invested in experienced buyers, and encouraged those buyers to invest the time in building supplier relationships. I was ill-prepared for the situation I faced ten years later in the same building.

The buyer who greeted me was far from experienced; in fact, it was her first job out of college. She did not have the time to develop a relationship and brusquely explained that she was under pressure "to wrap things up this afternoon." Five minutes into the call it was clear she knew little about the products she was buying. When I asked what I could do to help, she asked me to position my products against my competition. I took out a blank sheet of paper, drew some circles, one for each of my competitors, and positioned my product against their products. She snapped a quick look at her watch and announced that she had run out of time. Thinking that this had not been much of a call, I nervously asked what her buying intentions were. She replied, "Look, you explained who you are relative to your competition in a way that I find totally believable, so I'm ready to do my buying." She went on to tell me that only I and one of my competitors were getting orders. Noting my surprise at her sudden rush to judgment, she added, "It doesn't take a rocket scientist to see that competition in your category is brutal, so you wouldn't be sitting here if you didn't have a good product."

Here was her buying formula: She had replaced weeks of relationship building and hours of developing a product understanding with a few minutes of understanding the competitors in my product category. Her assumption was that in categories where tough competition assured quality and good pricing, a deep understanding of products and suppliers was superfluous. Knowing the competitive nature of the players within a product category was basis enough to make a good buying decision.

While this was an extreme case, I hear everywhere that buyers in general do not have the time to build relationships or understand product the way they once did. They are under pressure to make more decisions on more products of ever-greater complexity. Understanding the difference between competitors in a category is one way buyers cut to the chase and get more done in less time. In this sound-bite selling environment, the ability to skillfully position your product against your competition and in the mind of your client is the way to win business. As one experienced buyer told me, "Don't tell me who you are, I know who you are, tell me how you're different."

OLD THINKING	Sell the unique features of your product and don't mention your competition unless your client brings them up.

WHAT'S DIFFERENT	Customers are bombarded with information about your product and your competitor's. To cope, buyers must try to make sense of conflicting sales messages.

NEW THINKING	Positioning, a word once heard only in the marketing department, is now an essential part of face-to-face selling. Constructively comparing yourself to your competition is a basic skill.

Approaches

POSITION YOUR PRODUCT AMONG YOUR COMPETITORS

When I started on the advertising sales staff of *Broadcast Engineering* magazine, we were the number-two magazine in our market. *BM/E* (*Broadcast Management/Engineering*) magazine had been the leader for as long as anyone could remember. Our staff was much younger and sometimes we seemed a bit like kids who had stumbled into a grown-up party.

My publisher Cam Bishop hated the idea of being number two and researched the market carefully to explore how *Broadcast Engineering* could be repositioned to make us a better buy. At the time both magazines were aimed at both engineers and managers at TV stations. Surprisingly Bishop discovered engineers did most of the product purchasing. Thus he repositioned our magazine content to focus on just engineering. At first, my clients reacted badly. One said to me, "Josh, I'm used to getting two ice-cream cones"—managers and engineers—"and now you are telling me I can only get one?"

But I soon found that by positioning *Broadcast Engineering* as *the* engineering media buy I could undermine *BM/E*'s current position. First I had to convince—I mean *really* convince—a buyer that *Broadcast Engineering* was *the* one way to reach the real buyers, the engineers.

Here's how the plan worked: Once Broadcast Engineering was positioned in my customer's mind as *the* engineering magazine for the industry, when the *BM/E* salesperson paid a call and talked about how *BM/E* reached both engineers and managers, a red flag would go up in the buyer's head. He would think, "Hey! *Broadcast Engineering* owns the engineering position, so maybe you aren't so great with the engineers." This happens because the human mind hates inconsistencies and tries hard to resolve them. Suddenly the *BM/E* rep was having a hard time making the engineering side of his position stick. Here's the best part: The harder the *BM/E* rep pushed to sell the engineering side of the engineering and management position, the more doubt was cast in the buyer's mind about the magazine's ability to reach both markets.

In time, *Broadcast Engineering* passed *BM/E* to become the top magazine in its market. *BM/E* never fully recovered from having its positioning compromised and eventually went out of business.

POSITION YOUR CATEGORY

I once sold to a company that supplied power backup systems to many different industries. A buyer, concerned that my product was of interest to just one of those industries, told me, "Look, I don't know if I need your product because I don't know if I even want to sell into your industry." In this case, the way my product stacked up against my competitors' was of little importance unless the industry I was representing stacked up well against the other industries. The key to making this sale was to position the industry my product was useful in against other potential industries.

One way to position industries against each other is by contrasting how money is made in each and then segueing into an explanation of how the client's product fits in. For example, I contrasted three markets where a manufacturer of video equipment could sell video cameras in this way:

The cable TV industry:

1. *How money is made:* by selling monthly subscriptions to cable subscribers

2. *How cameras are used:* to produce local events or local TV commercials

The broadcast TV industry:

1. *How money is made:* by selling advertising airtime

2. *How cameras are used:* to produce local news and TV commercials for advertisers who don't have their own production capabilities

The teleproduction industry:

1. *How money is made:* by selling services to people who are looking to produce or create video programming

2. *How cameras are used:* by renting cameras along with operators to clients who want to produce programs

I have also positioned industries against each other by citing government statistics of the overall size of the market, and contrasting trends that are moving the markets. Then I bring the discussion back to the client's product or service and how it fits in.

REPOSITION A COMPETITOR

The key to repositioning a competitor is to redefine their key strength as a weakness.

I once had a competitor reposition a product I was selling. My product was clearly the quality leader in a market where quality could be accurately measured. Despite a major downturn in business, my company continued to aggressively raise prices. As my customers' business slowed they began watching every penny and were far from happy about our stiff rate increases. That our competition decided not to increase their prices only made matters worse.

A smart competitor capitalized on the situation. They openly admitted that we had the highest-quality product, but citing the hard economic times and our apparent insensitivity to their effect on our customers, repositioned us from the high-quality magazine to the greedy, out-of-touch-with-reality magazine.

Here, their positioning work countered my best selling efforts. When I would talk about high quality, my customers had been set up to think, "Yeah, and overpriced and greedy."

Step-by-Step

1. ESTABLISH A PRODUCT "POSITION"

When you position a product you are creating a way to describe your product and planting it in the customer's mind. You'll need to explain your product so it makes sense to a customer in the context of what he or she already knows about competing products, and the overall market they fit into. Your customer's mind isn't a blank slate. In the marketing classic *Positioning: The Battle for Your Mind,* marketing gurus Al Ries and Jack Trout write, "The basic approach to positioning is not to create something new and different, but to manipulate what's already up there in the mind, to retie the connections that already exist."

2. USING POSITIONING ON A SALES CALL

As a salesperson, the most common positioning presentation I make is to place my product against my competitors' in my product category. The challenge is to help your client understand your product category in spite of competing companies' conflicting claims. You don't have to resolve conflicting claims but at least acknowledge them. For example, in the story recounted above, both *BM/E* and *Broadcast Engineering* magazines claimed to reach broadcast engineers. In the course of positioning my magazine, I never tried to deny that *BM/E* covered broadcast engineers. Acknowledge your competitor's claims; the selling comes later.

The act of comparing your product to your competition alone usually won't result in a sale. This kind of comparison is the "one" of a one-two punch. It establishes the differences between you and your competition. Then you have to sell your customer by working those differences to your advantage.

When you make the comparisons it is impotant to be objective about the strengths and weaknesses of all products. You are trying to show how these products are different, not how your product is better. Objective comparison does the following:

A. By listing the product differences objectively and calling attention to them, small differences can take on greater significance.

B. An objective comparison will bring out how your client looks for value in your product category.

C. It flushes out your client's latent feelings about your competitors and their products.

D. It gives you a road map to your customer's mind.

What emerges from this dialogue is a comparative position for your product that might sound something like this:

Of all the electrical connectors, ours takes the least time to install.

Our factory is closer to your warehouse than any other manufacturer's.

Of all the audio magazines, ours reaches the most technical audience.

If you can own a position in your customer's mind as the connector that's quickest to install, the closest factory, or the magazine that's the best way to reach a technical audience, the next step is to continue the dialogue to show why this is important for your customers.

3. DO YOUR HOMEWORK

To position your product well you need to do some prep work. Start by answering the following questions:

A. How are we different?

If your customer sees little difference between your product and a competitor's, you are not going to be able to establish a unique position for your product in his mind. The product you sell will always seem more unique to you than it does to your customers. Positioning is a way to reinforce the differences.

Product differences don't lie in features alone. Sometimes product features aren't nearly as important as the way you do business.

In 1913, Alfred C. Fuller started a brush-making company that eventually distributed its brushes door-to-door nationally.

Fuller Brush salesmen became commonplace, and in 1932, the company sold a whopping $15 million worth of brushes. Alfred Fuller's brushes may have been slightly different from the brushes sold in stores, but what made the difference to customers was their distribution. Fuller differentiated his brushes through his delivery system, not by product features.

Aside from product features, price, and distribution, products and services can also be differentiated by:

extra service

reputation

faster response

extra diagnostics

extra information

leadership

product acceptance

specialization

craftsmanship

packaging

sales staff professionalism

marketing/advertising

future-proofing

educational service or content

design/styling

value-added extras

brand

concern for the environment or a cause

Says Lou Pritchett, former vice president of sales at Procter & Gamble, "Sometimes it's not enough to do things better. Lots of companies can do things better. The way you add real value is to figure out how to do things differently."

B. Who does my client think is my competition?

I once arrived on a call expecting to position my product against my two most serious competitors. My client stopped me not two minutes into my presentation and said, "You don't have to concern yourself with the first one. We used to give them business but we had a falling-out. As for the second, we have never considered them an option." My client then told me that he was considering buying from several competitors in another field and I adjusted my presentation accordingly.

In today's market you just don't know who your next competitor might be. Making assumptions is dangerous. It is simple enough to ask your customer, "Who do you think my competition is?"

C. How is my competition presenting themselves in my territory?

When I heard that a competitor was presenting themselves as the most reliable product in the market, I started working countermeasures into my sales talks. I presented the case for my product's reliability in a very matter-of-fact way, while positioning anyone who really had to push hard on this subject of reliability as someone who might have something to hide. The more my competitor pushed the message "We are reliable," the more often my customers thought, "What are you hiding?"

You will establish a stronger position if you borrow from

your sales competitor's scripts when you talk about their products. You don't have to advocate their entire position, but if what you say is supported by others who call on your client, it will stay with them.

4. THE POSITIONING PRESENTATION

A. Pursue a dialogue

As a salesperson, you have a real advantage over your counterparts in the marketing department because you can develop a customized position in face-to-face meetings. While the principles of positioning remain the same, this personal aspect makes your positioning far more powerful because you can tailor it to fit individual customers.

During your presentation it is important to keep asking for feedback to see if your customer agrees with what you have said so far. I always like to ask, "Do you see it this way?" or "Is this your understanding?" before moving on the next point.

B. Present the differences side by side

One way I like to start a presentation is with a clean sheet of paper and develop the list of competitors together with my client. I then list attributes and strengths under each product. When we are done with the lists we discuss the comparative strengths and weakness of all the competitive products in the market (from my customer's point of view) using the guide that we worked up together. If several competitors have overlapping attributes that are important, I might draw overlapping circles to illustrate the point. Eventually the unique attributes of my product inevitably emerge. When I am presenting to a new buyer who is unfamiliar with my market, I often just show up with a prepared chart and explain my point of view.

Typically you won't make a sale simply by showing or developing a positioning chart. The chart provides a way to focus the dialogue on the options available. The goal is to offer an honest side-by-side comparison of available products and stimulate a detailed and honest dialogue about how your client feels about each competitor and each attribute. Along the way you may uncover things you need to explain further, prove, or improve before the dialogue can move ahead.

C. Positioning scripts

There are infinite ways to position your products. Some examples:

1. Position against a leader

In markets where there is a dominant leader you often won't make a sale unless your product compares favorably with the leader. I never present a positioning like this as a one-on-one shoot-out. I always include at least one or two other competitors so it doesn't look like a hatchet job. Your presentation should be comparative not competitive. I grant the market leader superiority in terms of market acceptance but go on to win points in other areas.

By comparing several products along many parameters, you can often shatter the mystique of market leadership.

Positioning Statement: "My company offers almost everything the market leader does but can offer better customization because of our smaller size."

2. Position across technical specs

Customers may be uncomfortable listening to you slam the competition, but they typically like seeing comparative information. This is especially true in technical buying, where specs can be compared side by side. Says Mike Massari, procurement manager at Videotek, "When a new supplier comes to me I like to give him the part number that we are currently using and ask him for a side-by-side comparison of the specs. This tells me a lot and I enjoy working through the comparisons."

Positioning statement: "Of all the processors on the market today, our processors have the most inputs."

3. Position with specialization

Here you present your company and your competitors' and talk about who specializes in what. If you are a law firm trying to secure a client, you might talk about the kinds of cases competing firms have earned a reputation for winning.

Positioning statement: Of the law firms in your area, we have the best track record in intellectual-property cases.

4. Position across every competitor's unique strengths

Here you present the strongest possible case for buying your product *and* for your competitors'. Crazy? Actually it makes a very powerful presentation but you really have to know your competition very well to pull it off.

You might say something like, "Competitor A has the best credit terms, Competitor B has the best dealer network, and we have the best on-time delivery record." Then you go on to explain why on-time delivery is the most important virtue. You could be selling to a company about to initiate a "just in time" inventory management system in which the "on time" component is essential. The essence of this approach to positioning is to name your competitors and say, "Wonderful, wonderful . . . but for someone else."

Positioning statement: "We offer the best credit services for smaller companies like yours. Sure, Competitor A is a terrific alternative, but for larger companies."

5. *Positioning with demonstration*

A salesperson who sold electrical connectors found that his connectors could be installed more quickly than his competitors'. His positioning idea was to demonstrate his product in use, pulling in the performance differences as he went. It went like this:

"Our company makes the electrical connector that is fastest to install. Let's look at Company A. They have been in the connector business the longest and have the widest range of products. But it takes twice as long to install their connectors. Let me show you." (The salesperson took out two pieces of wire and Company A's connector and started snapping them together.) "It's a good solid connector but has not taken advantage of newer materials now available. You can see it took about ten seconds longer to install. And now for Company B. These folks have the least expensive connectors but they take three times as long to use. Let me show you." *Click!* "Now, here is our company's connector. We will never be the cheapest but we are the fastest to use." Out comes the wire and connector. *Click!* "See how the pieces fit together? And you're done in half the time."

During the presentation the salesperson talked about how faster connectors can mean efficient and profitable work for a contracting firm who uses them. After that, every time a salesperson from Company B proclaimed, "Mine is cheaper," the customer heard a voice in his head say, "And slower, too."

Positioning statement: "Of all the connectors out there, ours take the least time to install."

5. MAKING POSITIONING STICK

Some product positioning sticks better than others. Here are some tips to help make yours stick:

A. It must make sense within the context of everything else in your client's mind including your competitors' claims. To do this you must accept that some of your competitors' claims are valid and are also going to stick in your client's mind.

B. It must show how your product is different. Unless your positioning is based on a real difference, you and your competitors will occupy the same position. You'll have gained nothing.

C. It must be based on a deeper truth about your product or about doing business with your company so that the message is reinforced even when you are not there.

D. Don't base your position on superlatives. When you position your product you are describing how it is different. Unless you can prove this in a specific, measurable way, eschew the words "best," "quality," and "reliability."

E. It must be simple.

Reality Check

WHAT IF THEY DON'T BUY MY POSITIONING?

I have seen many salespeople fail to establish their product's position because they confuse positioning with making a product pitch. Here are the relevant differences:

Product pitch:	Positioning presentation:
Starts with your product	Starts with your client's perception
Focuses on how your product is better	Focuses on how your product is different

Is product-centered	Is category- or market-centered
Discredits competitors' strengths	Acknowledges competitors' strengths
Leaves a product-specific impression	Leaves an impression of how the product compares with all alternatives

The hardest part of this is for salespeople to acknowledge competitors' strengths and learn how to use or counter them to their advantage.

Application Question

How can I position my product against those of my competitors in a way that creates preference for my product?

16

Motivating Your Customer by
Offering Proof

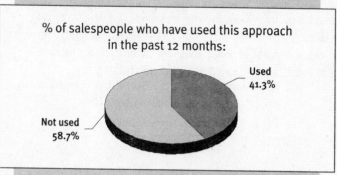

% of salespeople who have used this approach
in the past 12 months:

Used
41.3%

Not used
58.7%

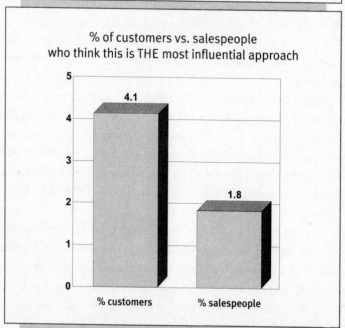

% of customers vs. salespeople
who think this is THE most influential approach

4.1

1.8

% customers   % salespeople

"What a buyer really wants is proof. Instead of just making a claim, back it up with something, even if it's just anecdotal information. Weak proof is better than no proof at all."

KEVIN FITZGERALD, editor in chief, *Purchasing* magazine

"I like to buy from people who come in, put the facts on the table, and let the facts sell themselves. People who know the most about what they are selling, and pressure you the least, are the ones you end up trusting."

MICHAEL RACZ, president of RDA International

During my first swing through a new territory I heard a lot about Jack, who sold in the same territory for the competition. He had lived in the area for ten years and tied up most of the business.

At first, I had trouble even getting appointments. Whenever I referred to information I'd researched about my competition, my clients would say, "Oh! Jack isn't going to like that," or, "I wonder what Jack will say when I tell him what you just said." By the time I returned to my office to make follow-up calls, Jack had already been in touch with every client I visited, countering my facts with his facts.

Six months later I had made little progress and felt ridiculous. I really did have a better product, but Jack exerted such influence over his customers that not one of them would believe me. A senior co-worker said sympathetically, "Look Josh, he has a ten-year head start on you, there is nothing you can do. It's an in-bed situation."

I realized I would never win a relationship-building contest, but firmly convinced that I had the better product, I rethought what I could say or do to convince the customers. Presenting the facts simply did not make any difference because Jack would quickly counter again with his facts. Then I thought, "What if I could *prove* my product was better in a test specific to the customer's situation?" I devised a way to survey my customers' customers to see how they felt about my product versus Jack's. My boss, desperate for progress, agreed to fund the test.

My first attempts failed, as Jack got wind of my plan and convinced his friends that such tests were ridiculous. Finally a client at a small account told me, "You're a pain in the neck, Gordon. I'll do the test, and when Jack's product wins I never want to hear from you again." We did the test and Jack's product lost big. My client was stunned and began to question where his allegiance belonged—to Jack or to his own company. When my client announced he would switch suppliers and buy from me, Jack went nuts. I held my breath as he went several rungs above my client's head and met with the owner of the company. But the owner saw that his customers clearly preferred my product. The test was the key to the sale.

In the wake of my small victory I developed a new strategy. I decided not to compete with Jack on a personal level, but instead to present myself as a helper trying to arrange and pay for customer product tests. When the results of the next few tests for major customers clearly favored my product, word spread like wildfire throughout my territory. Jack's influence began to fade.

Give me a better product and a solid way to prove it any day.

OLD THINKING   If you can just get in and present the facts, your customer will be sold.

- -

WHAT'S DIFFERENT   Today, information is a commodity and every-one has facts to support their point of view. Buyers have little time to navigate a path through a sea of conflicting information.

NEW THINKING   It is not enough to present the facts; you have to prove them in a way that is meaningful.

Approaches

PROVE IT WITH A CUSTOMER TEST

Customers are always looking for proof specific to their situation. If you can give it to them it makes their job that much easier. In many technical selling situations there is an engineering department that routinely tests and approves any purchase. If a large sale hangs the balance, arranging for a customer test may be the key to getting the business. Testing is far more common than most salespeople realize. Consider the upside of the following scenarios:

■ To test the appeal of a new shampoo it's shelved next to big brands in one of a nationwide chain of stores . . . If the store's customers prefer it over current offerings, the chain might decide to pick it up and distribute it nationally.

■ A client tests an ad agency by contracting a small direct-mail campaign . . . If the campaign is more successful than similar efforts conducted by the current agency, bigger jobs could be just around the corner.

■ A radio station surveys the customers at a chain of health clubs to see which radio stations they listen to . . . If the survey shows club patrons listen to that particular station, they've made a compelling argument for a large advertising contract.

- An information technology manager tests a new software application on a limited basis . . . If the test is successful, the software could become a standard throughout his network.

The ultimate proof that your customer will be well satisfied if he buys from you is to test your product with his system, customers, personnel, or processes.

If arranging customer tests were easy, salespeople would do far more of them. But a customer test can disrupt your client's business and be an imposition on her time as well. Even a simple testing means tapping into your client's internal resources. Even asking for your client's assistance to do work that helps you prove your point is tricky. Some clients simply refuse, thinking there's little reason to help you do your job.

Here are some tips on selling the idea of a customer test:

1. Develop a test that reveals something besides preference for your product

The U.S. division of a Japanese lens manufacturer wanted to expand its offerings in the U.S. market to include smaller scale lenses that accommodated the newer, lighter-weight professional cameras. I offered to sponsor a survey at their booth at a major trade show to help them find out just how much business they were losing by not offering the lighter lenses. In addition to a question about carrying these newer lenses, I asked a preference question about the product I was trying to sell. The booth personnel, looking for ways to convince the home office in Japan that they needed these new lenses, were passionate about getting this survey done and got virtually every booth visitor to fill out a questionnaire. When the booth visitors voted solidly for the new lenses as well as for my product, we all went home happy.

2. Make it turnkey

The best testing programs can be instituted with a minimum of effort from your client. Give us access to the store shelf and we'll do the rest. Give us your customer mailing list to test and we will do the rest, etc.

3. Pay for it

Never forget who is buying and who is selling. If you are doing the test to help sell your product, then you should cover the expenses. There is a hidden benefit to this. If you are paying for the test, then you have some influence over specifically what gets tested and how, both of which can greatly affect the outcome.

4. Ask up front if you can share the results with others

If you go through the expense of testing your shampoo at one supermarket chain, can you share the results with other retailers? Some clients will agree to this out of respect for the trouble and expense you are incurring; others will ask for the entire project to be proprietary, but the question is always worth asking.

5. Explain why testing is important and how best to do it

I worked at a videotape production facility that housed a duplication lab. We used thousands of videocassettes every week, yet the testing for purchasing new blank tapes was haphazard at best. José, the chief engineer, would buy some new tape and try it in the recording machines. If it didn't jam, he would buy more. If a random tape did jam we stopped buying that brand and switched to another. Now, most videotape jams are caused by inadequate machine maintenance, not bad tape.

I always felt the tape manufacturers who called on us missed out on the opportunity to educate us on better methods of testing their products. Sometimes you have to tell people how to measure quality for your product, explain why it is advantageous, and give them the tools to do it.

6. Establish an ongoing customer proof program

The best use of customer proof is to publicize a standing offer industry-wide. You will conduct a customer test anywhere at any time to prove your product is best. I have seen several clients use this approach successfully. It works like a guarantee of quality. Surprisingly few customers actually take advantage of it. The ones who do help perpetuate the perception of your product's superiority in the minds of all who don't.

EVIDENCE

Evidence is information you share that supports your point of view. If you provide evidence for your point of view and your competition does not, you often win the sale. A customer once told me, "When you were in my office I was convinced I should buy from you. When your competitor came into my office I was convinced I should buy from him. After you both left I sat down to make my decision. You had documented the points you made and he didn't, so you got the order."

Evidence you can gather to use on a call:

- Testimonials. If you have a very happy customer, ask him to express his very happy feelings on paper.

- Information from the financial community. You would be surprised how much is available on the Internet at financial Web sites.

- Articles from magazines and newspapers. Again, go to the Web. There is a ton of information a mouse click away.

- Your customer list. This can be evidence of customer acceptance or market leadership.

- Product specifications

- Awards your product or company has won

- Information from a competitor. If you can get ahold of the selling package for the product you are selling against, you can contest specific advantages they claim. Often the most influential evidence you can produce comes from your competition.

- Customer satisfaction surveys

PROVE IT BEFORE YOUR CUSTOMER'S OWN EYES

There's no better drama than proving your product's superiority right before your customer's eyes. I was competing against a second-rate trade magazine in the video industry that stayed in business by giving rave product reviews to any manufacturer who advertised. A reader paging through the publication would see a ridiculous parade of glowing product "puff pieces." Needless to say, the reviews were anything but credible. When I explained this to ad managers who were giving the magazine business, they reacted badly. They told me they loved the stellar reviews and wanted to keep them coming.

I realized I had to help them see this publication's editorial quality from their customers' point of view.

I bought a desktop publishing program and created a fictitious magazine called *Copy World*. Then I took each article from one issue of my competitor's magazine and translated it from the video industry to the "copy industry." Thus the article entitled "Sony Wins Over KMEX with New Cameras" became "Xerox Wins Over Kmart with New Copiers." I translated the content of this and other articles as well, keeping them pretty much intact. I found photos and ads of copiers and inserted them into the pages. On the last two pages I created an appendix that cross-referenced the titles of *Copy World* articles with their original names as they ran in my competitor's magazine.

I took my presentation to the biggest account in my industry and told him, "I know that you sell quality products and would never run your ads in an editorial environment that had no credibility. "Of course not," he agreed. I continued, "Let me show you an example of this kind of poor editorial product, from the photocopy industry." As I walked my client through the pages of *Copy World*, he was visibly repulsed. He said, "How do those people stay in business being so insensitive to their readers?" Then I said, "What if I told you that your company is now advertising in a magazine just like *Copy World*?"

His eyebrows shot up and he exclaimed, "That's impossible! Maybe some small division of my company that I've never heard about would do it." Then I turned to the cross-reference pages that revealed the ruse. His eyes widened and he stared at the pages for a few seconds, saying nothing. Then he threw his head back, laughed hysterically, and said, "Boy, you got me on this one!" I had proved my point.

PROVE IT WITH STORIES

Some salespeople use stories to prove their points. As they travel their territory they gather anecdotes about people associated with the field and share nonconfidential stories with buyers. Typically these stories are short and concern people they know. Here are the most common story scripts that I see salespeople use and ways you can use them for your own products.

The success story

This is a story about how another company bought your product or service with successful results. I personalize success stories by adding, "Yes, this is the way they now do it at the Zebra Company. If you want to know more you can call my friend John White, who will be glad to tell you all about it." If the client agrees, I contact John White and tell him to expect a call.

Your own personal story of conversion

"When they approached me to sell this product, I thought, "Hey, I've been buying this product for years, of course I can sell it." Or: "When I was first approached to sell this product, I was very skeptical. I told them I had never heard of your company, why should I work for you? But then they explained . . ."

The conversion-of-a-significant-peer story

This script mirrors the preceding one but focuses on how a significant peer came to buy your product. It begins, "At first he was skeptical but then . . ."

The story of how your product was created

Every product has a story. Often the best way to describe it is to describe how it came into being. "Years ago, a brilliant scientist saw the need for keeping his feet warm while ice skating and invented the first . . ."

The application story

Describe how another company implemented use of your product. Here you use the story to explain the steps in implementing your product. I have often used stories of this kind to make doing business with me seem easy. "Some people think

that switching suppliers is hard but I just helped Monroe Industries do it. The general manager there was worried that a
lot of things could slip through the cracks, so I sat down and
we went over a checklist . . ."

Conversion of a competitor

Recount how a customer who was buying from a competitor
switched allegiances. "Finally he said, 'Why am I paying all this
money just so my ad agency can have a fancy front office and
take us on a celebrity golf outing every year . . . ?' " It's a great
way to make competitive points without doing the criticizing
yourself.

The best way to come up with stories is to keep your ears
open and gather them yourself. Stories about my own territory
are often the most convincing.

PROVE IT WITH SURVEYS

Sometimes your product advantage is intangible: better customer service, better acceptance among your customers' customers, wider acceptance of your product versus another,
evidence of higher customer satisfaction, etc.

The good news is that any attitude, perception, preference,
or feeling can be measured through surveys. The bad news is
that you cannot accurately survey any of the above for the future. Often selling is about convincing a customer that she will
have a positive experience in the future. While you cannot accurately survey the future, you can survey existing attitudes that
indicate what a buying experience might be like.

If 92 percent of first-time buyers have a positive feeling about
your product versus only 32 percent for your competition, it is
logical to assume that buying from you will result in a better
experience.

Step-by-Step

1. WHAT YOU HAVE TO PROVE IN GENERAL

There are many things you can say on a call that need no backup. If you were to say your company is painting their office building blue or that you have a new VP of internal affairs, you need not offer proof.

But statements that compare the benefits of doing business with your company versus a competitor's or statements that describe what a customer experience might be like after he buys from you cry out for proof. Every buyer knows that your job is to sell and a good buyer should measure your words carefully. On these subjects, general claims asserted without any backup are often ignored. "We have the highest quality, best delivery times, best technology, etc." are typically written off as meaningless to buyers.

2. FIND OUT WHAT IT IS YOU NEED TO PROVE TO MAKE A SALE

In every competitive selling situation there are at least two points of view. Help your customers assign greater value to your products with pertinent evidence or proof. Consider:

- You sell a processor that runs on less power . . . Your competition sells a processor that uses more power but runs at a faster speed.

If you can prove that lower power consumption is most important for your client's specific situation, you could win the sale.

- You sell a vacation package that includes two Caribbean countries in seven days . . . Your competition sells a package that includes five Caribbean countries in seven days.

If you can prove to a corporate sponsor that their people would rather spend more time getting to know fewer locations, you could win the sale.

■ You sell a product that is built to last longer . . . Your competitor sells a product that is cheaper.

If you can prove that longer lasting is better you could win the sale.

In this situation, as in any situation involving price benefit, if your product does not have the lowest price, you will need proof that it is better in some way that makes up for the additional cost.

3. FIND OUT WHAT KIND OF PROOF IS REAL FOR YOUR CUSTOMER

Proof is many things to many people. I had a client so focused on a single dominant competitor that the only proof that was "real" to him related to what his competition was doing. If his competition was using my product, that was "proof" enough for him to buy. Some clients like research and some don't. Some take marketplace acceptance as proof (i.e., more people use this software than any other), and some don't.

The most convincing proof is delivered on your customer's terms. The best way to discover which way to go is to simply ask your customer, "What would it take to prove to you that my product is better?"

4. SET THE STAGE

I once took the initiative and tested a new client's customers on my own. Through a friend on his sales staff I obtained a customer list, did a survey, and discovered that his customers preferred my product over the product his company was then buying by a wide margin. I thought I would impress my new client and make a big sale. He didn't take the news well and blasted my survey. He nitpicked every aspect of the methodology and told me it was seriously flawed. I quickly slipped the study back into my bag.

In a year's time I got to know this client better. During a call he interrupted my presentation to tell me he was considering buying from me but he had to weigh all his evidence carefully. Switching suppliers, he explained, was not something that was done on a whim. It seemed that he needed one more thing to push him over the edge. I asked, "We did a study on your customers before you got here, do you remember seeing it?" He told me that he didn't. I pulled out the same year-old survey and walked him through it. It made a big impression and I closed a substantial order.

People believe what they want to believe and proof is only proof when your client is ready to accept it. Many salespeople present proof too early in the conversation. Proof should not be introduced until after you have established what sort of information is meaningful for your customer and whether he is ready to consider it.

5. PRESENTING THE PROOF

Standing all by itself, proof is less persuasive than you might think. On a sales call, you'll make the greatest impact when it is used as the "punch line" of your presentation, not its central theme. For example, when you are presenting an impressive list of current satisfied customers, first have a discussion about how important widespread acceptance is for a product in your category. You may be dealing in a networked situation where the more people who use your product, the greater its impact. Or you might be selling in an industry in which a few large distributors (all of whom are on your customer list) control a majority of the business.

When your customer agrees with your premise, then present your customer list as proof of your product's significance. If you present the customer list without the introduction, your customer might ask, "So what?"

6. PUT IT ON PAPER

If it's not on paper it's just hearsay. Once you put your proof on paper, it can be distributed to committees, checked by third parties, even shown to your competitors for comment. Your evidence carries tremendous emotional weight once it is put in black-and-white.

Reality Check

WHAT IF THEY DON'T BUY YOUR PROOF?

If your customer does not "buy" your proof, ask him why. Here are a few of the most common reactions and ways to respond:

"I think your methodology is flawed."

When I sold research in New York, customers would often raise methodology issues, but when I went on to sell other products, I realized that most customers don't know beans about methodology. When customers raise this issue they are most often telling you one of two things:

1. *"I don't agree with the premise of your survey."*

If the survey methodology is over my head, I try to get the dialogue to focus on what the survey is saying. "I understand you think the study is flawed, but what about the point the survey makes. Do you disagree with it?"

2. "I don't trust you completely and think you may have manipulated the results."

This gets back to trust. Go back to chapter 3. If your customer really is interested in the study methodology, listen to his concerns carefully, take notes, then consult with someone who can answer his concerns. Then get back to him.

Other times I have carefully collected magazine articles as evidence only to have the customer object: "So you are showing me an article that says HD television is coming soon, so what? Yesterday I read an article in *USA Today* about how it won't hit the market for years."

What I shoot for is a level playing field. Both sides may well be valid, but on which do you want to take a position? Then I go on to argue my point of view.

Finally, if a customer doesn't buy your proof, move on. The beauty of offering proof to help make a sale is that if your customer doesn't buy it, you can always bring different evidence next time. Take your shot and move on.

Application Question

How can I prove what I am saying is true in a way that is meaningful for my customer?

17

Motivating Your Customer by
Explaining Cost

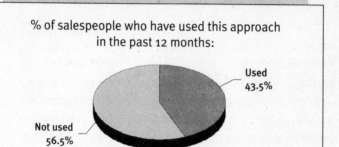

% of salespeople who have used this approach
in the past 12 months:

Used
43.5%

Not used
56.5%

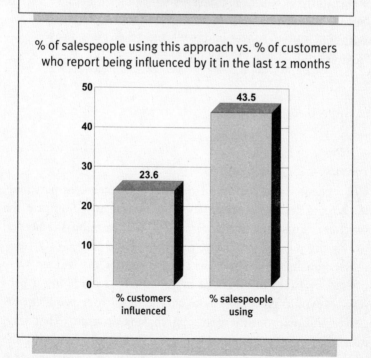

% of salespeople using this approach vs. % of customers
who report being influenced by it in the last 12 months

23.6 — % customers influenced

43.5 — % salespeople using

"In markets where competitive prices are a given, the new way to differentiate yourself is by looking at overall cost. Here you are selling the business model you operate under to deliver better overall cost even though, in some cases, the price of products you sell may be higher. It's about selling a unique business model, not 5 percent off the price."

JEFF RAIKES, executive group vice president,
worldwide sales and marketing, Microsoft

"Whether we need a part-time secretary or a billion dollars' worth of computer chips, we procure on the Internet. We can scan across a supplier base globally and ask why this widget in Singapore costs more than the same widget in Hungary. The power of the buyer is strengthened because he can scan across a large base of acquisition and have a more constructive conversation with the seller. As a sales executive, this scares the hell out of me."

BILL ETHERINGTON, senior vice president and group executive,
sales and distribution, IBM

A client wanted to buy from me, but because of personnel cuts at her company she had no one to administer the purchase. To set up the program she had in mind she needed to buy my product and three others over the course of a year.

Recognizing that the other three products she wanted were offered by other divisions of my company, I made her a proposal. I would personally take charge of all four product purchases and map out the year's purchasing program. That way, instead of submitting monthly approvals for each purchase, she could go to her boss once for pre-approval on a yearlong program. I would simplify her billing so that only one bill (not four) from one company (mine) would arrive on her desk each month. She only had to sign off on one monthly bill against a preapproved program. By convincing her to do some internal planning and consolidating of suppliers, I saved my client the cost of a part-time administrator and made myself a sale.

The strategic advantage I used had little to do with the competitive features of my product and much more to do with my company's overall business model. I was able to make the offer because my company had a more comprehensive line of products than my competitors. Played out at a large corporation, this scenario can create a huge incentive to buy by offering savings of millions.

Offering economic incentives to motivate customers to buy is nothing new, but it looks a lot different today than it did when I started selling. Years ago the only real economic incentive was lower pricing. But as more product procurement moves to the Internet and large, consolidated customers and buying groups get involved in price negotiation, lower prices are becoming commonplace. Widespread low pricing eventually leads to price flattening. Price flattening means that the difference between the lowest price and the highest price any customer pays in a market becomes negligible. As a result price becomes less of a differentiator.

But as buying products becomes more complex, new ways of offering economic incentives emerge. For example, you can make compelling presentations by explaining the "total cost of ownership" of a product over its lifetime.

Studies done at information technology centers have tracked the cost of buying a single computer and compared it with the total cost of owning that computer as part of a company network. It turns out that buying the actual computer is only 20 to 30 percent of the "total cost of ownership" for the computer's life. The rest of the expense comes from maintaining technical support, system administration, and maintenance. A salesperson who can demonstrate ways to reduce these internal costs can create a powerful economic incentive to buy.

When you have explained your product's ability to reduce costs in this fashion, your customer might say, "So your prices are the same or maybe a bit higher than your competition, but if I buy from you my overall costs go down."

OLD THINKING	If you sell value hard enough, price will not be an issue.
WHAT'S DIFFERENT	Low prices are an issue. Internet procurement programs and the buying power of consolidated customers and buying groups have intensified the demand for low prices. They've become commonplace.
NEW THINKING	As prices flatten they become less of a differentiator. Presenting ways to reduce overall costs is the new way to offer economic incentives to do business.

Approaches

EXPLAIN "TOTAL COST OF OWNERSHIP"

You can often motivate a customer to buy a product that represents a large capital expenditure by shifting his attention off the initial purchase price to focus on the total cost of ownership over the product's life span.

According to Jerry Cohen, director of product marketing at Vinten Inc., the price of a camera robotic system his company sells to a large TV station is around $300,000. But the system enables one operator to control all the cameras in a studio, eliminating the need for three full-time camera operators. While the initial price of the system might seem high, when you factor in the cost savings, the "total cost of ownership" over a two-year period is virtually free.

Using the "total cost of ownership" approach is very popular in high-tech sales, where faster systems, which can deliver greater efficiencies, can be cost justified over a specific period of time.

EXPLAIN "TOTAL COST OF ACQUISITION"

When you're selling commodities or semicommodities on an ongoing basis, there is a big difference between price and cost. Kevin Fitzgerald, editor in chief of *Purchasing* magazine, says, "Price is what you pay. Cost is your expense to do what you want to do with the thing you paid the price for. And that includes everything from processing the order to shipping, storing, handling, and disposing of waste."

Determining the total cost of acquisition means examining all costs associated with the purchase and use of your product to see if there are ways to reduce them. Says Fitzgerald, "If you're buying three different products from three different suppliers and you're able to buy all three products from one supplier, it's possible that the latter is the better deal. The actual purchase price could be a little higher for those products, but your total cost could go down. That's because of all the other hidden soft costs that go with managing three suppliers versus one. Ordering from three, paying three, having different deliveries from three. A salesperson can made big points by showing a purchaser how they can reduce or even control total costs."

WORK ON A COST-REDUCTION PROGRAM

With large-volume customers you can propose working together on a cost-reduction program. First sit down and examine both companies' operations to see if there are ways to coordinate or integrate functions to achieve cost savings. Ideally you'll gain a competitive advantage and still be able to offer solid pricing.

Initiating a cost-reduction program requires complete understanding of both your own and your customer's operations and costs. These are some of the ways cost efficiencies can be achieved:

Combining pickups and deliveries

Joint inventory management

Automating to reduce the cost of processing transactions

Developing stocking programs

Upgrading to faster systems

Upgrading to more cost-effective materials

Streamlining operations

Says Fitzgerald, "The most important thing to remember, and one both suppliers and buyers often forget, is that real cost savings come from reducing costs—not price. When costs are the point under examination, reducing them benefits both the buyer and supplier."

Step-by-Step

1. FIND OUT WHAT YOUR COMPETITORS ARE CHARGING

Cost-based selling is a given in a competitive environment. You will gain no advantage with a cost reduction proposal that is routinely undercut by a competitor. Often you can monitor your competitor's pricing by visiting their Web site or regularly asking friendly customers to pass on their pricing literature or proposals.

2. LOOK FOR THE COST OPPORTUNITY

Cost opportunities can be found in the nature of your product, your business model, or your customer's business model. For some salespeople cost opportunity is obvious—i.e., their product was created as a cost-saving process, service, or device.

With an understanding of your business model's impact on your customer's operations, you can take this motivational strategy one step further. Says John Kinnaird, vice president, general manager, Preferred Account Division at Dell Computer, "In the beginning, people really didn't understand the direct selling model for computers. They figured if they called on the telephone they'd get a better deal. In the beginning they were right, but we have since developed the direct model into having more advantages than just price." For example, Kinnaird explains that selling direct enables a company to coordinate the nationwide delivery of a computer system from a central point of origin.

Ask yourself, "What makes doing business with my company *different and better* than doing business with my competition?" These are some typical advantages:

Logistics: Our service locations or factories are closer.

Size: Our product breadth is wider.

Specialization: We have unique specialized knowledge.

Speed: We do it faster, saving you time and money.

Centralization: We can control inventories or information at one location.

Distribution: We can deliver to end users more efficiently.

Remote control: We can minimize the need for "truck rolls" or visits to end users.

Highly reliable: You can use us to create "just-in-time" delivery programs to control your inventory more effectively.

3. TELL THEM THE "SAVINGS STORY"

If you tell your customer you can offer lower overall cost, his first question will undoubtedly be, "How?" He needs to hear that you are not offering substandard products or services but instead have real ways to offer cost savings. You need to explain where the savings are coming from in your business model. If you are selling in a competitive environment, you can then compare this aspect of your business with how your competition does it. For example:

- Because we do transactions on the Internet, our transaction costs are much lower.

- Because we sell direct, we can save the money that normally goes to middlemen.

- Because we operate in less expensive locations, our operational costs are lower.

- Because we spend more on store security, we control theft and pass the savings on.

- Because we price to induce more frequent buying, we make our profit on volume.

Your rationale may be very specific to your product and industry.

4. SHOW COST MODELS

You can make your cost benefit tangible by showing your customer an economic model of the cost savings under discussion. One way to do this is to show your customer examples of the cost savings another happy customer has achieved. If you can't get permission to share this kind of financial data, create models for a variety of facilities. Jerry Cohen's salespeople at Vinten have three financial scenarios they use that outline typical costs saved at small, medium, and larger TV stations. A big-city TV station's expenses and cost savings will be very different from those at a small-town station.

5. DO YOUR CLIENT'S NUMBERS

If your client is ready to take the dialogue to the next level, you will want to build a model of overall cost savings specific to her situation. Be sure to ask for the details you need to proceed. Often these scenarios are most persuasive when their benefits are described over several years. I have seen presentations in which:

- A single sheet of page summarized all the details

- The numbers were crunched out on a spreadsheet

- A five-year program was presented on five sheets of paper, one page laying out the cost savings for each year

- A time line was used to map cost savings

Reality check

WHAT IF YOU HAVE A CRAZY COMPETITOR WHO WILL MATCH ANY COST ADVANTAGE YOU PRESENT WITH A LOWER PRICE EVEN IF IT MEANS HE OR SHE IS LOSING MONEY?

I have worked against crazy competitors who would rather lose money on a proposal than let me get business. If your competitors fit this description, it is best to make a preemptive strike and anticipate a price attack against your cost-savings proposal.

To do this you need to add a little extra to your "savings story" (see Step 3). Your goal is to make your competitor's price attack appear illegitimate. As you explain how you can achieve a cost advantage, mention in passing that none of your competitors is in a position to offer this, and that if a competitor does offer it, he is probably losing money just to get the bid away from you. Then ask your customer how well their company treats customers whose business they lose money on. While every customer likes getting a lower price, no customer wants to be treated as burdensome business.

Essentially, you're suggesting that anyone who can't explain why their price is lower should be treated with suspicion. Consider what Frank Will Smith wrote in *Beyond the Swivel Chair* back in 1940: "Cheapness is a come-on that succeeds but not for long unless it is backed up with honesty, quality, service, and resale. And cheapness generally does not carry these factors. We men who sell are human; we naturally welcome a lower price than our competitor, but a lower price carries a responsibility with it. The discerning buyer is quite apt to ask why our price is lower, and unless we can convince him through honest sales exposition that quality, dependability, and service have not been sacrificed, our price advantage may not get us the order."

Application Question

How can I present a way of doing business with my customer that will result in lowering the "total cost of ownership" of my product?

My Top Ten Lessons

While writing this book I was a New York City–based salesperson with a full territory of clients, quotas, and deadlines. As I would shift from interviewing the greatest sales minds of our time back to selling my own customers, I was challenged to measure the ideas I was hearing against my actual selling experiences. As a result, writing this book was not merely an intellectual exercise, I lived it. It was a journey, and at its conclusion these are the ten biggest lessons I've learned:

LESSON #1: IT IS MORE IMPORTANT TO BE WELL TRUSTED THAN WELL LIKED.

In a world of repeat purchases, consolidated buying, interdependencies, and partnerships, greater power may have shifted to the buyer but so has greater risk. When risk to the buyer increases, customers make buying from someone they trust their top priority.

Given the limited time and resources you get to spend with any of your customers, how big a priority is trust building? Most salespeople jump at the chance to build a personal rela-

tionship with a customer and invest considerable time and resources to do so. But trust-building opportunities, such as
aggressively handling mistakes or missionary selling before buying begins, are often overlooked. It is important to identify
trust-building moments, strategies, and codes of behavior and
to pursue them as your highest priority.

LESSON #2: YOU HAVE TO CREATE VALUE, NOT JUST TALK ABOUT IT.

I used to ask myself what I was going to *say* on my next
sales call. Today I ask what am I going to *do*. Customers are
less interested in spending time with salespeople who just add
a positive spin and offer to buy lunch over information that
customers can download from the Internet themselves. Today
a sales call has to be more than presenting information; it needs
to be about planning, researching, thinking, brainstorming, idea
sharing, knowledge building, value creating, and discovery.

LESSON #3: THERE ARE BIGGER DIFFERENCES BETWEEN HOW YOU AND YOUR COMPETITION HANDLE CUSTOMERS THAN BETWEEN YOUR PRODUCTS.

Your job is to live your product and as a result you will see
greater differences between your product and your competition
than your customers ever will. But today there are many other
ways to work with customers that did not exist before. Customers may be seeing less and less differences between product
offerings, but they are seeing greater differences in how salespeople and companies build and maintain relationships and customer interfaces.

LESSON #4: YOU SELL TO A CUSTOMER NETWORK, NOT A COLLECTION OF ISOLATED CUSTOMERS.

Your customers are more connected to each other than ever before. Through chat rooms on the Internet, e-mail, partnerships between members of your customer base, and newsgroups, you sell in a networked world. Assume that if you do something truly outstanding, either positive or negative, all of your customers will hear about it and be influenced.

LESSON #5: INFORMATION IS A COMMODITY. KNOWLEDGE IS POWER.

The old adage "information is power" predates the Internet. Customers can now access more information than ever and make informed decisions without ever talking to a salesperson. What now has value is the knowledge, judgment, experience, and training to help your customer take advantage of the ubiquitous information.

LESSON #6: YOU WILL SELL MORE AS AN AGENT OF CHANGE THAN AS AN AGENT SELLING PRODUCTS.

Salespeople have always been an agent of change. The job is to change nonbuyers into buyers and buyers into greater or more loyal buyers. As such, the status quo is your enemy. But this idea takes on far greater importance when you are selling in a market where change is fast and constant. In the corner of the world affected by your product you can lead change, draft along with change, or get hurt by change. As a salesperson, it is essential to know what trends affect your business and to embrace them.

LESSON #7: YOU ARE YOUR CLIENT'S PERSONAL BRAND MANAGER.

The two most important parts of your brand are its promise and its delivery on that promise. For your customer, you are the key to both. Individual products, corporate logos, and letterheads can change every year but the key to winning and growing business over time is to manage the perception of your company and make sure it delivers consistently to your customer. This means managing your company's brand on a one-to-one level.

LESSON #8: CUSTOMER LOYALTY IS THE RESULT OF BETTER CUSTOMER STRATEGY, NOT BETTER CUSTOMER SERVICE.

Excellent customer service has never been more important. It has also never been more common. Today, excellent customer service is only your admission to the game. The bigger question is, what do you do when you arrive on the playing field? Salespeople who invest time in creating unique customer experiences, strategically shape their customer relationships, and build multilevel relationships between their organizations have the best chance at customer loyalty.

LESSON #9: IT IS EASIER TO DIFFERENTIATE YOUR PRODUCT IN THE FUTURE THAN IN THE PRESENT.

In times of rapid change customers want to know that what you sell them today will stay current and maintain support in the future. The differences in how you and your competition propose to do this five years out can be more varied, interesting, and compelling than the differences between your current product offerings, which are limited by the rigidity of present-day reality.

LESSON #10: THE BIGGEST SALES WILL GO TO THE MOST AGGRESSIVE CUSTOMER MOTIVATORS, NOT THE MOST AGGRESSIVE CUSTOMER PUSHERS.

What has not changed is that aggressive salespeople still make the most sales. What has changed is how the aggression is channeled. Customers are smarter and just won't stand for the aggressive "closer" style salesperson of old. But if you use a motivational approach, your customer will view your activities as aggressively working for them. Stop pushing products, start motivating your customer to buy.

I would like to end this chapter, and this book, with the question that started me on this project: How do you motivate your customers to buy from you?

Finding answers to this question is a process, not a technique. The process begins by putting your customers first and developing a deep understanding of their goals and needs. But the real magic comes when you merge the specifics of your company's offerings with the specifics of your customer's needs in a customer dialogue. Keeping this question in the back of your mind can help you stay focused on your customer while moving toward a sale. By contrast, if the guiding question in the back of your mind is, "How can I sell more this month than last month?" you will put your need to make a sale first and miss many sales opportunities.

For every customer there is a unique motivational approach; your job is to find it.

Your Customers Are Changing . . . Are You?

Findings from the *Selling 2.0* survey of Sellers and Buyers

I n order to become a true "customer motivator" you need to understand how your customer thinks. A national survey* conducted as part of the writing of this book revealed that the attitudes of customers on subjects of persuasion, trust building, and loyalty during the selling process have changed significantly, while attitudes among salespeople have not.

Many salespeople are less effective today because they believe "conventional wisdom" on how customers are *supposed* to think that is simply out-of-date.

---

*The *Selling 2.0* survey of sellers and buyers compared attitudes between salespeople and customers and was the result of a 2,500-piece mail survey. Lists of salespeople came from *Selling Power* and *Sales & Marketing Management* magazines. A list of customers was obtained from Dun and Bradstreet. The survey was conducted between November 1999 and January 2000. 452 usable responses were received for a response rate of 18.4 percent.

1. WHICH MOTIVATIONAL APPROACHES ARE MOST PERSUASIVE?

Salespeople believe that relationship building is the most persuasive approach by a wide margin. Problem solving was their second pick, followed by building trust.

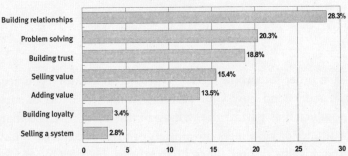

Which ONE motivational approach is most persuasive?
Salespeople say:

Approach	Percentage
Building relationships	28.3%
Problem solving	20.3%
Building trust	18.8%
Selling value	15.4%
Adding value	13.5%
Building loyalty	3.4%
Selling a system	2.8%

While customers and salespeople picked the same top six approaches, they ranked them very differently. Customers selected building trust as their top choice by a wide margin. Relationship building—the top choice among salespeople—followed a distant second.

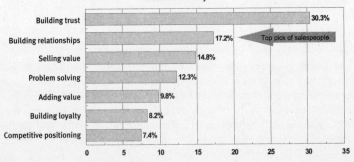

Which ONE motivational approach is most persuasive?
Customers say:

Approach	Percentage
Building trust	30.3%
Building relationships	17.2% — Top pick of salespeople
Selling value	14.8%
Problem solving	12.3%
Adding value	9.8%
Building loyalty	8.2%
Competitive positioning	7.4%

Salespeople versus customers:

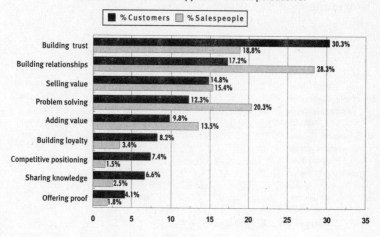

Which ONE motivational approach is most persuasive?

■ % Customers ☐ % Salespeople

Building trust	30.3% / 18.8%
Building relationships	17.2% / 28.3%
Selling value	14.8% / 15.4%
Problem solving	12.3% / 20.3%
Adding value	9.8% / 13.5%
Building loyalty	8.2% / 3.4%
Competitive positioning	7.4% / 1.5%
Sharing knowledge	6.6% / 2.5%
Offering proof	4.1% / 1.8%

Conclusions:

1. In the new economy, it is more important to be well trusted than well liked.

2. From the customer's point of view, salespeople underestimate the persuasive power of building trust, addressing competitive positioning, sharing knowledge, and offering proof.

3. Salespeople may overestimate the persuasive ability of building relationships, adding value, and problem solving.

2. WHICH CHARACTERISTICS OF SALESPEOPLE WIN THE TRUST OF CUSTOMERS?

Salespeople believe that being a good listener is the top way to win the trust of customers.

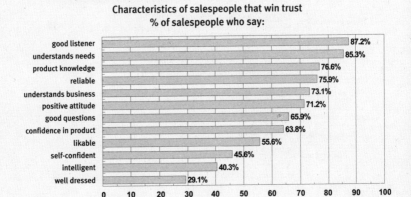

Characteristics of salespeople that win trust
% of salespeople who say:

While customers agree with many of the top choices of salespeople, they give being a good listener a relatively low rating.

Characteristics of salespeople that win trust
% of customers who say:

Salespeople versus customers:

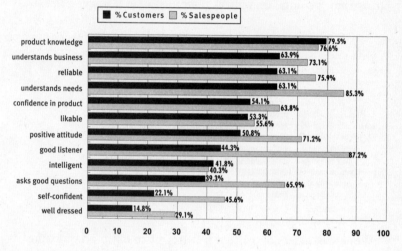

Characteristics of salespeople that win trust

■ % Customers □ % Salespeople

product knowledge	79.5% / 76.6%
understands business	63.9% / 73.1%
reliable	63.1% / 75.9%
understands needs	63.1% / 85.3%
confidence in product	54.1% / 63.8%
likable	53.3% / 55.6%
positive attitude	50.8% / 71.2%
good listener	44.3% / 87.2%
intelligent	41.8% / 40.3%
asks good questions	39.3% / 65.9%
self-confident	22.1% / 45.6%
well dressed	14.8% / 29.1%

Conclusions:

1. Knowledge and understanding, not asking questions or listening, is what most makes customers trust salespeople. While knowledge and understanding may be the *result* of good listening and question asking, they alone are not the trust builders salespeople think they are. If a salesperson asks a lot of questions and no understanding develops, trust is lost.

2. Salespeople greatly overestimate the trust-building power of a positive attitude, dressing well, and acting confidently. Although no one can disagree that these are very important to customers, building trust is a deeper and more serious activity.

3. ON CUSTOMER LOYALTY: WHY DO SALESPEOPLE LOSE CUSTOMERS?

Salespeople believe that the top reason they lose business, by far, is that a competitor offers their customer a lower price.

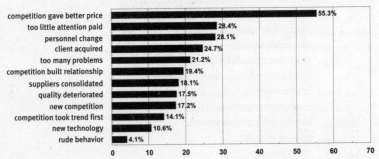

Reasons why salespeople have lost business in past 12 months
% of salespeople who say:

While customers agree that a better price often accompanies switching suppliers, they see far more variables as being important in motivating them.

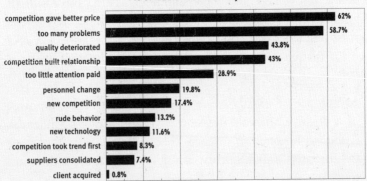

Reasons why salespeople have lost business in past 12 months
% of customers who say:

Salespeople versus customers:

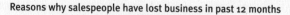

Reasons why salespeople have lost business in past 12 months

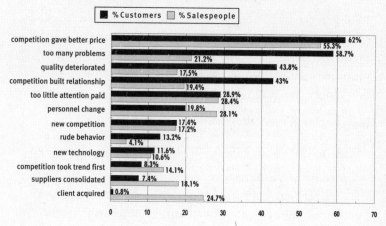

Salespeople often do not get the "whole picture" when they lose an account. It is often easier for a departing customer to tell the salesperson that the competition gave them a super-cheap deal and move on. But there are areas that customers rated as very important in speeding their departure that salespeople greatly underestimate.

Here are the conclusions:

1. Competitive pricing is important to keep customers loyal but so are three other areas that salespeople often under-estimate.

First: Immediate problem solving

58.7 percent of customers reported changing suppliers be-cause of too many problems, while only 21.2 percent of sales-people report losing customers because of this. Oops! Beyond a point, many customers simply don't tell you about the problems they are having with you, they just move on. See chapter 6 on Solving Problems.

Second: Deteriorating quality

43.8 percent of customers report changing suppliers because of deteriorating quality, while only 17.5 percent of salespeople report losing customers because of this. Oops! Are your customers sold on the overall quality of your products? Sometimes this gets taken for granted.

See chapter 8 on Selling Value.

Third: Competition built a better relationship

43 percent of customers report switching suppliers because the competition built a better relationship, while only 19.4 percent of salespeople report losing customers because of this. Oops! It is important to monitor your competition's relationship-building activities.

See chapter 10 on Building Relationships.

4. WHICH APPROACHES ARE SALESPEOPLE MOST EFFECTIVE AT DELIVERING?

Salespeople use the 17 motivational approaches covered in this book often, but to different degrees.

Motivational approaches used by salespeople in past 12 months

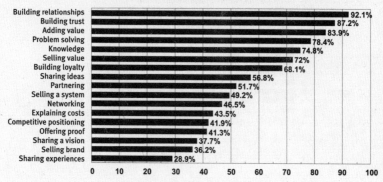

Motivational approaches EXPERIENCED BY CUSTOMERS in past 12 months

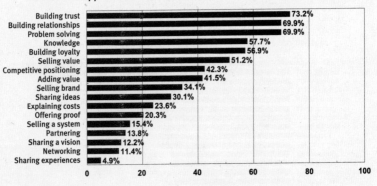

Customers acknowledge that they are influenced by these approaches, but not to the same degree that salespeople using them in the field report. It seems that there is a lot of "nondelivery" of these approaches. For example, 78.4 percent of salespeople say they add value when they make sales calls, but only 41.5 percent of customers say they experience being motivated to buy by salespeople using this approach. Sometimes just using an approach on a call does not make it effective or real for a customer. Overall, customers report the experience of being motivated to buy by the use of these approaches well below salespeople.

Salespeople versus customers:
Motivational approaches used/experienced in past 12 months

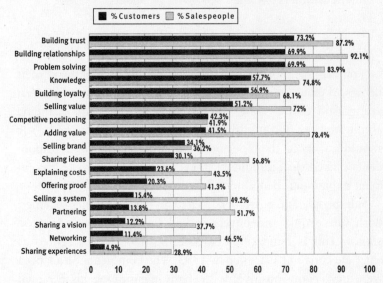

Several approaches may receive low ratings among customers because salespeople are being selective in their use. For example, not every customer is appropriate for a partnering agreement, a networking sell, or a system sell. If salespeople don't widely use the approach, then customers as a whole will report its effectiveness less often.

But the shortfall in "delivery" occurs on approaches that salespeople typically use often—specifically, adding value, sharing a vision, and offering proof. Just because these are presented to a client does not mean they are seen as real or persuasive.

Conclusions:

1. Salespeople are most effective when they are solving problems.

2. Salespeople need to be more effective when they are adding or selling value, offering proof, and selling a vision. In

these areas more salespeople believe they are being persuasive than customers say they are being persuaded.

5. WHO IS THE GREATEST SALESPERSON OF OUR TIME?

You can tell a lot about a group of people by looking at their heroes. Asking salespeople and customers who is the "greatest salesperson of our time" reveals how attitudes are changing about what an accomplished salesperson is and how he or she should go about their business. For this reason, after respondents picked their candidate, they were asked to write a comment explaining their choice.

Salespeople and customers picked an overall winner together: Both salespeople and buyers picked Lee Iacocca as their top choice. This is remarkable considering that Iacocca retired as chief executive at Chrysler in 1993. The comments on Iacocca were universally positive, with many mentioning his personal charisma and credibility as well as his achievements in the Chrysler Corporation turnaround.

Typical comments included: *He said what he was going to do and did it . . . He turned around the third-largest carmaker . . . I picked him because of his vision, and power of persuasion . . . He sold a bad company to a nation and changed it . . . Through personal charisma and foresight he changed the automotive industry.*

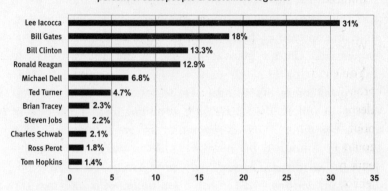

Who is the greatest salesperson of our time?
percent of salespeople & customers together

The salespeople's choice:

Salespeople and buyers differed on their number-two pick. Salespeople picked Ronald Reagan. The comments for Reagan focused on his personal credibility, communication skills, and charisma.

Typical comments: *He was a great charismatic leader with very strong persuasive skills . . . He was the "great communicator" . . . Got people to change their attitudes about themselves, a great communicator . . . Persuasive, credible . . . Communicated ideas, attitude, and confidence better than any of the others.*

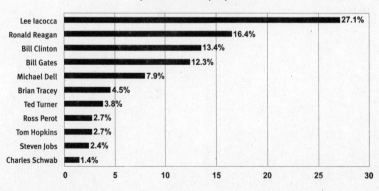

Who is the greatest salesperson of our time?
percent of salespeople

The customers' choice:

In contrast, the overwhelming second choice among buyers was Bill Gates. Here, the comments were overwhelmingly positive, but instead of focusing on personal characteristics, they emphasized Gates's innovation, vision, and ability to create value.

Typical comments included: *He seems to always be one step ahead . . . Innovative . . . He built an empire by selling the value of the computer . . . He is the master, he built something from nothing . . . Look at his success . . . He took an idea, created a product, surrounded himself with good people, made his product better, and marketed it into a multibillion-dollar business.*

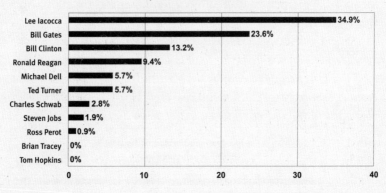

Who is the greatest salesperson of our time?
percent of customers

Lee Iacocca	34.9%
Bill Gates	23.6%
Bill Clinton	13.2%
Ronald Reagan	9.4%
Michael Dell	5.7%
Ted Turner	5.7%
Charles Schwab	2.8%
Steven Jobs	1.9%
Ross Perot	0.9%
Brian Tracey	0%
Tom Hopkins	0%

Salespeople versus customers:

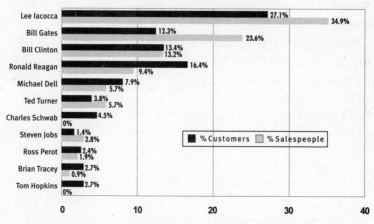

Who is the greatest salesperson of our time?
percent of salespeople versus customers:

Lee Iacocca — 27.1% / 34.9%
Bill Gates — 12.3% / 23.6%
Bill Clinton — 13.4% / 13.2%
Ronald Reagan — 16.4% / 9.4%
Michael Dell — 7.9% / 5.7%
Ted Turner — 3.8% / 5.7%
Charles Schwab — 4.5% / 0%
Steven Jobs — 1.4% / 2.8%
Ross Perot — 2.4% / 1.9%
Brian Tracey — 2.7% / 0.9%
Tom Hopkins — 2.7% / 0%

■ % Customers ☐ % Salespeople

0   10   20   30   40

Here we have a contrast in expectations as to what a salesperson should do. When asked who epitomizes the height of accomplishment in the selling craft, salespeople leaned toward qualities of personal persuasiveness (Reagan), while buyers looked more toward innovation and value creation (Gates), with Lee Iacocca, the top choice, possessing both.

When customers rated candidates highly they mentioned the creation of new products or services. With Iacocca it was the Mustang and mini-van; with Gates it was the Windows operating system; with Turner, CNN; with Schwab, on-line financial services.

When salespeople gave high ratings there were mentions of personal charisma and persuasiveness. These comments were especially common among those who picked Reagan, Iacocca, Clinton, and Jobs. This message from customers to salespeople says: charisma is fine, but create more value for us.

At the start of chapter 11, Creating Value, spin-selling guru

Neil Rackham tells us the big issue for companies today is to convert their sales staffs from value communicators to value creators. Is Bill Gates the role model for the next generation of customer motivators? One vice president of purchasing who chose Bill Gates wrote, "He's not flashy, but he gets the job done."

As we move to the future, customers will demand salespeople who can "do something," on a sales call, not just offer a positive spin and offer to buy lunch.

Index